THE CANADIAN PATIENT'S BOOK OF RIGHTS

A Consumer's Guide to Canadian Health Law

▪ **Revised and Updated** ▪

Other Books by the Author

Canadian Hospital Law: A Practical Guide (Toronto: Canadian Hospital Assn., 1974)

Canadian Manual on Hospital By-laws, with W.M. Dunlop (Toronto: Canadian Hospital Assn., 1976)

Canadian Hospital Law, 2nd edition (Ottawa: Canadian Hospital Assn., 1979)

The Canadian Patient's Book of Rights (Toronto: Doubleday, 1980)

Legal Sex, with F.A. Rozovsky (Toronto: Doubleday, 1982)

Canadian Health Facilities Law Guide, with F.A. Rozovsky (Don Mills, Ont.: CCH Canadian Ltd., 1983 with monthly supplements)

Canadian Law of Patient Records, with F.A. Rozovsky (Toronto: Butterworths, 1984)

Canadian Dental Law (Toronto: Butterworths, 1987)

The Canadian Law of Consent to Treatment, with F.A. Rozovsky (Toronto: Butterworths, 1990)

Canadian Health Information: A Legal and Risk Management Guide, 2nd edition, with F.A. Rozovsky (Toronto: Butterworths, 1992)

AIDS and Canadian Law, with F.A. Rozovsky (Toronto: Butterworths, 1992)

Home Health Care Law: Liability and Risk Management, with F.A. Rozovsky (Boston: Little, Brown and Co., 1993)

Medical Staff Credentialing: A Practical Guide, with F.A. Rozovsky and L.M. Harpster (Chicago: American Hospital Publishing, 1993)

THE CANADIAN PATIENT'S BOOK OF RIGHTS

A Consumer's Guide to Canadian Health Law

■

Revised and Updated

Lorne E. Rozovsky, Q.C.

Doubleday Canada Limited

WARNING!
This book is intended to assist the reader to better understand those areas of the law that may affect his or her rights as a patient. It does not replace advice given by a lawyer that is specific to a particular set of circumstances and as governed by local legislation and local law generally. Because the law is constantly changing and because each case requires specific advice from a lawyer, the reader should not rely on this book for legal advice.

Canadian Cataloguing in Publication Data
Rozovsky, Lorne Elkin, 1942–
      The Canadian patient's book of rights

Rev. and updated.
ISBN 0-385-25449-0

1. Patients - Legal status, laws, etc. - Canada.
2. Sick - Legal status, laws, etc. - Canada.
3. Medical laws and legislation - Canada.
I. Title.

KE3648.R68 1994   344.71'0321   C94-930573-1
KF3823.R68 1994

Cover and text design by David Montle
Printed and bound in Canada
Printed on ∞ acid-free paper

Published in Canada by
Doubleday Canada Limited
105 Bond Street
Toronto, Ontario
M5B 1Y3

To Andrews Kwame Pianim
of Accra, Ghana,
friend and scholar,
in admiration of his courage,
wisdom and leadership in
human rights and dignity.

ACKNOWLEDGEMENTS

Many thanks to my colleague and friend, Juanita Swinamer of Lefar Health Associates, Inc. in Halifax for her research, patience and encouragement; and the support, interest and advice of my wife, Fay, and our two sons, Aaron and Joshua. On the Doubleday Canada side of the desk, special thanks to Susan Folkins who has guided me through the development of this second edition, John Pearce who started me on the road and Marlene Fraser whose efforts have brought this book to many who need it the most.

CONTENTS

HOW
TO USE
THIS
BOOK

MOST PEOPLE ARE from time to time patients. Illness both serious and not so serious strikes all of us. And as members of society we are all affected by the law. Every minute of our lives, the law has an implication on what we do. It governs our relations with our friends, our colleagues, our families, our communities and our governments. When we are both patients and members of society, some special and interesting legal implications arise. It is this combination that this book is all about.

This is not a book for academic and philosophical research. It avoids the use of complicated legal terms that are thrown about by lawyers and judges who themselves do not always understand them, thus creating the basis for more disputes and courtroom battles.

It does not analyze court decisions and compare them word for word. In other words, it is not a legal text. If readers want in-depth discussion of particular points of health law, the Additional Reading section at the back lists most of the books that are currently in print in Canada on the subject of health law. Cases are named more by way of examples, to illustrate that real cases involving real people went before real Canadian courts. Readers who are interested in reading the decisions of the judges in those cases should take the name of the case, the year and the name of the court to a law librarian or to a friendly lawyer who will be able to look it up.

Because provinces and territories and the federal government are constantly introducing and changing acts and regulations, and because these differ across the country, this book does not provide details of individual acts or regulations, which will be of no practical use to patients anywhere else in the country. So often legal texts use one province, usually Ontario, as an example on the assumption that all other governments will follow. This is not always the case. The other problem is that any mention of a particular piece of legislation can be seriously misleading, since by the time this book is being read, the legislation might well have changed.

What the book does try to do is to make the reader aware of the basic principles of patients' rights, and the types of subjects affecting patients that have been dealt with by the courts and by governments. It is hoped that this will encourage patients to be aware that they have or may have legal rights in certain situations. Patients must be encouraged to ask questions and become better informed. A knowledgeable patient is a patient who is in a better position to work with health care professionals and facilities in obtaining health services.

It is hoped that patients reading this book will gain an understanding of their relationship with health professionals. Whether doctors, dentists, nurses, physiotherapists, respiratory therapists or medical technologists, these people are trained to think in terms of what is wrong with the patient, what can be done about it and how. They are not trained to think in terms of legal rights and duties. If they were, they would find it very difficult to carry out their function. They think of patient needs, but needs as determined by health professionals, not as determined by the patient.

Lawyers, on the other hand, are not trained to think of what patients need. They think in terms of what patients *want*, whether they have a right to what they want and whether someone has a legal duty to give it to them. As a result, health professionals and lawyers are frequently at odds with each other.

It is not, it must be said, that health professionals are actively denying patients their legal rights. Legal rights are simply not their primary concern. So intent are health professionals on providing care or treatment that patients may often unintentionally be denied their rights.

What patients and health professionals must understand is that patients have both health needs and legal rights and that these two must go together. Because health professionals are not unaware of patients' rights but rather are not concentrating on them, it is important that patients have an understanding of what their basic rights are or might be, and make these known in their dealings with the health care system.

If patients want to know the specifics of the law affecting them, legal advice is a necessity. This book should help patients become aware of when they might wish to seek legal advice; it will not tell them how to sue their doctor, hospital, psychologist or anyone else.

With the knowledge to be gained by reading this book, situations that may lead to a deprivation of rights can be avoided or at least minimized. A courtroom battle may keep lawyers and judges employed. It may grab the attention of the media. But considering the human cost, one wonders whether anyone ever truly wins, doctors, nurses, hospitals... or patients.

Lorne E. Rozovsky

PART
ONE

1

THE

RIGHT TO

HEALTH

CARE

CANADIANS READ HORROR STORIES about patients who are left ill and dying at the doorsteps of American hospitals. We hear of American doctors turning their backs on the sick and the injured. In Europe this would be a crime. In America, many Canadians believe, it is part of the health care business. No money, no insurance, no service. Canadians also believe that American patients may be refused care because of the fear of a malpractice suit.

These are Canadian myths. At one time they were true, but not any longer. In a true emergency or for women in active labor, American hospitals are required to at least evaluate and where appropriate to stabilize or treat the patient, though they may not be required to do more than that.

And the issue of whether a patient has such a right has not been dealt with in reported Canadian court decisions.

Canadians are frequently denied admission to hospital, but not for financial reasons. Unless it can clearly be shown that the admission is not medically necessary, the cost is covered by the provincial hospital insurance plan. Admission could be denied to a long-term-care facility on a financial basis, though most provinces have some system of covering costs for those who cannot afford them. The coverage for long-term care and the rapidly expanding home care services is far less comprehensive than hospital insurance. As a result, services might well be refused on this basis. The same is true of the growing number of uninsured health care services, such as private physiotherapy, psychology and chiropractic services. Insured prescription drug services are also being cut back.

What many Canadians do not realize is that the law in this country is not always clear. Traditionally, there was no absolute legal right to health care in a hospital, in a nursing home or from a physician, dentist or anyone else. To overcome this problem, many provinces created a right at least to hospital care.

Yet even this right often has so many exceptions that patients can be refused admission — and in fact *are* refused. Invariably, however, this refusal is due to lack of accommodation rather than lack of money. With governments across the country forcing hospitals to reduce their number of beds, refusal on these grounds will become even more frequent. A hospital cannot offer what it does not have.

The Hospital Act in British Columbia, for example, states that no person suffering from a communicable disease requiring isolation shall be admitted to a hospital unless there are accommodation and facilities for isolation. On the other hand, it states that no hospital shall refuse to admit a person on account of his indigent circumstances. (Nowhere does it define indigent circumstances.) The act prohibits admission to a hospital except on the order of the hospital's board of management or someone authorized by the board. In effect, this means that hospital personnel must approve the admission. It is not the sole prerogative of the patient's physician. The legislation does not, therefore, guarantee a right to hospital services.

Some provinces do appear to establish a right to admission. The Hospitals Act of Nova Scotia requires that the administrator of a hospital admit patients. Even this, however, does not establish an absolute right of a patient to be admitted. First of all, accommodation must be available. Second, a physician either with a dentist or alone must apply for the admission of the patient, stating that the patient is in need of hospital services. Third, any right under this provision is subject to the conditions and regulations prescribed by the board by-laws.

In Ontario, the Public Hospitals Act requires that a hospital accept a patient who has been admitted by a physician under the regulations. The regulations simply say that admission must be medically necessary.

Despite the fact that many of these legislative provisions seem to give a patient a legal right to be admitted, patients are constantly refused admission to hospital. They are refused admission because there are no beds available, or at least no beds in the service the patient requires. They may be refused admission because there is no operating room time available. The realities, therefore, make nonsense of provincial legislation.

It may be argued that if hospitals were operated more efficiently in this country, services would be available. Many services are not available on weekends or in off-hours except in cases of emergency. This of course creates a backlog of patients during the regular weekday hours. Again the reality is that hospitals are not operated efficiently. And there is little government incentive for them to do so, since their budgets would be cut to correspond to any savings the hospitals might make. The current financial restraints may result in cuts in services rather than improved efficiency, unless the entire system is restructured.

Human rights legislation does not assist Canadians who want and may need health services. Human rights legislation aims to prevent discrimination on the basis of categories such as race, religion, nationality, physical or mental disability and in some provinces sexual orientation. The problem in Canada is that if one patient is being discriminated against in favour of another, it is not as a result of any of the characteristics mentioned in the legislation.

In some cases, it may be argued that patients with one type of illness have an easier time getting treatment than those with another type. This discrimination takes place because of the willingness or ability of an institution to provide services for the favoured illness to a greater degree than for the other. Whether this is a violation of human rights has not been tested in the courts. It would be very difficult, however, to show that this discrimination was directed towards a particular individual with a particular illness or, as the legislation calls it, disability.

If the Canadian Charter of Rights and Freedoms were to apply to hospitals, it would be an interesting argument that a patient has a constitutional right of life and security of the person to be admitted to a hospital, let alone a nursing home or any other facility. However, the courts have determined that the Charter does not apply to the operation of hospitals, nor would it apply to nursing homes or other health facilities.

The Charter does give every person a legal right to life, liberty and security of the person. None of these rights may be taken away except by following the rules of fundamental justice, that is, fairness. Canadians must look for other sources of legal rights as patients, such as provincial statutes and court decisions. Quebec may look to its statutes and its Civil Code.

For some time, Canadian hospitals have been forced to ration services because of the limited facilities available. This has resulted in extensive delays in treatment. Many Canadian patients are not receiving the care they require when they require it. The solution appears to lie not with the law but in the political forum.

Summary of Principles
1. Despite any provincial legislation to the contrary, Canadians do not have an absolute right to health services.
2. Any right to health services is subject to availability as determined by the facility providing those services.
3. There is no constitutional right to health services in Canada.

2

THE RIGHT
TO A DOCTOR
OF ONE'S
CHOICE

Medicine as a Business

MANY AMERICANS REFER TO the Canadian system of medical care as "socialized" medicine. In fact, nothing could be further from the truth. A more apt description would be "regulated" medicine. Canadian doctors are, on paper, one of the last bastions of free enterprise. Most Canadian physicians work for themselves. At least in theory, once a doctor has received a licence to practise in a province or territory, freedom to open up shop is virtually unlimited.

If there were no other considerations, doctors would be just as free as lawyers, dentists, plumbers and garage mechanics. Just as doctors are free to enter the competitive market, so too are patients free to shop around. No one assigns a patient to a doctor or a doctor to a patient. Many patients have no regular doctor and get medical services from whoever happens to be available. The same is true with dentists. Doctors and patients are in a competitive marketplace.

Restrictions on a Patient's Right to Know

The traditions of the medical profession discourage doctors from thinking of medical practice as a business. So, too, patients tend to think that doctors should not be motivated by the same drives as businesspeople. As a result, all of the health professions, from dentistry to chiropractic, have placed restraints on self-promotion, viewing it as undignified and unprofessional. Aggressive advertising, daily specials and give-aways for the first one hundred patients are prohibited. Advertising of a special technique "as approved by the famous Dr. X" or "as recommended in the *XYZ Journal*" is prohibited. A doctor, dentist or other health professional can be severely reprimanded by the disciplinary body governing their profession and may even lose the licence to practise by pursuing such business practices.

This not only restricts the rights of the professional, it also affects the rights of patients. If a patient wishes to find the surgeon who has performed the most cardiac bypass operations with the most success, the patient will have to rely on the word on the street. Much will depend on the family physician who makes the referral. This information is not publicized, and the surgeon who issues even the most tasteful advertisement saying that he is the best in town would be in severe trouble with the medical disciplinary body of the province and with his or her hospital. This restriction on advertising seriously affects the patient's right to make an informed choice of surgeon.

There are many theoretical reasons for such restrictions, one being that advertising of this sort may be taken out of context and could be misleading. That one surgeon has a higher success rate with a particular operation than another surgeon does not necessarily mean that the first surgeon is better. It may mean that that surgeon accepts only patients who are more likely to be successful, not necessarily all patients who need the operation. There are, of course, laws against misleading or false advertising.

The real reason for these restrictions is that medicine — and in fact all of the professions, including law and accounting — are considered above the crassness of commercialism. There is a fear of degrading the tradition of what has become known as "the profession." As a result, professional codes frequently restrict how large an advertisement can be, how often it may appear and what it may say. Even statements that are true may not necessarily be advertised to the public. Because of more conservative attitudes in Canada, most professions would not follow some of their American counterparts by allowing radio and television advertising, even though it is through those media that most of the population gets its information.

In the past ten years lawyers have moved sharply away from the restrictions against advertising on the grounds that potential clients should be able to make an informed choice and that lawyers should be able to give them sufficient information to do this. One wonders, of course, whether the expensive brochures now put out by many law firms in Canada really enhance the consumer's rights, or simply add to the cost of legal services.

Restrictions on the Number of Providers

The reality of Canadian life is that there are restrictions on the free market practice of medicine and other health professions. These restrictions, not to be confused with professional codes of conduct, stem from the fact that at least in medicine almost all services are paid for by government. In recent years these costs have been rising astronomically, even though Canadians are not any sicker than they were before.

It has come to the attention of government health authorities that the more doctors there are, the more medical services will be rendered, whether or not patients need those services. It is largely a matter of judgement as to whether a patient needs a medical service. In a great many cases, doing nothing would probably have no effect whatsoever on the patient. The illness or condition is going to get better either with or without a physician, or it is not.

The theory is that if there are fewer doctors, it will be more difficult to see a doctor. As a result, many patients will do without medical services, at enormous savings to government. The theory of course implies that if their condition becomes very serious, the patients will be able to see a doctor. It has not been explained how the very ill patient will be able to get to a doctor any more easily than the patient who is less seriously ill. The other argument against this position is that the progression to a serious ailment might have been prevented by early medical intervention. As with so many debates of this type, much depends on the particular patient and the circumstances.

However, governments are making increasing attempts to control how many doctors practise and where they practise. The idea is to keep them away from places where there are already lots of doctors and increase their numbers in geographic areas where there is a shortage. Attempts are also being made to alter the number of doctors in particular specialties.

Some may argue that free market competition would look after that. Because the patients do not pay for the services they receive, there is no restraint on patients going to doctors. The more doctors available, the more procedures will be performed, even for the same number of patients.

If government efforts are successful, the effect will be felt indirectly. No longer will patients have the right to see any doctor in their own community, since many doctors will not be permitted to practise in that community. So far, these government efforts have met legal roadblocks.

Governments have also tried to control who is permitted to bill the medicare program. This would mean that doctors could practise wherever they liked, but only a certain number in each community would be able to collect from the plan. Since Canadians are not likely to want to pay for medical services personally, any doctor outside the plan is not likely to attract patients. These efforts, too, have run into legal roadblocks, though eventually they are likely to be successful in some form. The result may very well be the payment of different rates to doctors practising in different areas, or supplements to practise in underserviced areas and disincentives in overserviced areas.

The result of these government initiatives will be that doctors will not have the right to practise where they wish, or at least will be discouraged from doing so. Patients will be restricted to doctors in their area except for emergencies or by referral. Patients will also be restricted in the number of physicians available to them.

Similar efforts are not directed at other health professionals, since their fees are not usually paid for by government health insurance. The market forces are therefore able to operate to a much greater extent. Even in these cases, however, government restrictions on the funding of training schools can restrict the number of professionals available, and thus restrict the patient's freedom of choice.

The Right to a Member of a Medical Staff

In order to be admitted and treated in a hospital, it is necessary to be admitted and treated by a physician who is a member of the medical staff of that hospital. A hospital admits, and allows for the care and treatment only of, patients who have been admitted by one of its own physicians and who are to be cared for by one of its own. A doctor may have a licence to practise medicine but does not automatically have the right to admit or treat patients in a hospital.

The right of a doctor to admit and treat patients in a particular hospital is not a legal right. It is a privilege for which the doctor must apply. It is given by the board of trustees or directors of the hospital when it appoints the doctor as a member of its medical staff. This is known as medical staff or hospital privileges.

An application must be made for various categories of medical staff membership, such as active, associate, courtesy or consulting. Each category carries with it certain rights. There may be the right to admit but not to treat a patient. There may be the right to treat a patient but only when called in by another physician as a consultant. A physician may also be required to take on various responsibilities in the hospital, such as attending a certain number of medical staff meetings, or attending in the emergency department or taking a number of continuing education courses every year.

There are also basic requirements for every physician who applies for privileges. These include a valid licence to practise medicine and may include certification in the specialty in which the doctor wishes to practise. A doctor may be required to hold membership in the Canadian Medical Protective Association, which will provide legal defence in case of a malpractice suit.

These requirements vary from hospital to hospital, depending on hospital by-laws and policies. Therefore, it may be possible for a doctor to have certain privileges in one hospital as, say, associate staff, but not the same privileges in another hospital even in a category of the same name. It is also possible for a doctor to be a member of the staff of more than one hospital, assuming that privileges have been granted in each. This may result in a doctor being able to perform certain types of surgery in one hospital but only able to assist another surgeon in another hospital.

Membership in the medical staff does not mean that the doctor is permitted to carry out all procedures. Appointment to a particular category is further restricted or delineated. This means that the doctor is given the privilege of carrying out only specified procedures, such as ear, nose and throat surgery but not abdominal surgery. A doctor may have psychiatric privileges but no obstetrical or surgical privileges. Minor surgical privileges may be granted, but not major procedures. A surgeon may be permitted to do certain procedures alone but only assist another surgeon in other procedures.

All of these restrictions have an effect on the patient. It means that a patient may be admitted by a family physician but cannot be treated by that physician if she or he does not have treatment privileges or does not have the type of privileges necessary to carry out treatment. Or a patient may have one procedure done by one doctor but may not be able to get the same doctor to carry out another procedure.

The fact that a doctor does not have privileges to carry out certain procedures or does not have privileges in a certain hospital does not necessarily mean that the doctor is not competent. It may mean that the doctor has not met certain educational standards required by that hospital. It may be that the hospital does not have the necessary facilities or staff to support the privileges the doctor is seeking. The hospital may not have enough trained personnel or the necessary equipment to provide the appropriate aftercare.

The hospital may also have a quota on the number of physicians or surgeons. By admitting a doctor to the medical staff, the hospital is really taking on not only that doctor but also that doctor's patients. The hospital may not have enough beds or operating rooms to service a larger number of potential patients.

Regardless of how competent a doctor may be, a doctor in a hospital must be a member of a hospital team consisting of other doctors and other health disciplines. Therefore, if a doctor cannot get along with others, or does not communicate well with nurses or technologists, the hospital may be forced to cancel that doctor's privileges. The patient then has no right to have that doctor in that hospital or to carry out procedures in that hospital.

The doctor may also not be able or willing to meet various hospital requirements quite apart from competence. In some hospitals, the doctor must live within a specified distance of the hospital so that emergency calls may be answered promptly. Attendance at meetings, continuing education sessions and service on hospital committees may also be required.

A history of malpractice claims or discipline proceedings may also prevent a doctor from obtaining privileges. A history of overusing hospital facilities, or having a history of poor results, may affect privileges.

Whereas the doctor has a right to a fair hearing before privileges are removed or restricted, the patient who wants that doctor in that hospital does not have any right before the hospital's board of trustees.

In British Columbia, Alberta, Manitoba, Ontario and Quebec, a doctor has a right to appeal to an outside board when decisions are made affecting privileges. The basis of the appeal and the authority of the appeal board vary from province to province. In some cases this right applies only to doctors who are already on the medical staff and whose privileges are not renewed or are removed, suspended or altered. In other cases it also applies to doctors who are not members of the medical staff but are applying for privileges. In a roundabout sort of way, this right to appeal assists the patients of that doctor who want their doctor to be able to practise in a particular hospital and to carry out certain procedures. The appeal boards have the right to overrule the hospital board. In some provinces there can be a further appeal to the courts.

In the other provinces there is no such right to appeal. The only right is that of the doctor to appeal to the courts on the basis that the decision of the hospital board was not arrived at in a correct manner. The board may not have followed the procedure that may exist in provincial legislation or in the by-laws of the hospital. The board may have ignored the principles of natural justice or fairness in making its decision. It may not have granted the doctor a fair hearing, or may have been biased in its decision making. The doctor may not have been permitted to bring legal counsel or witnesses, or may not have been permitted to cross-examine witnesses. The board may have based its decision on information or documents the doctor was not allowed to see.

Any of these grounds may prompt a court to declare the hospital board's decision invalid. Essentially, this is not a decision regarding patients' rights, but it does affect patients who wish their doctor to receive a fair hearing regarding privileges to treat them at a hospital for the services they want from that doctor.

There are situations in which a patient is in an emergency situation in a hospital. The patient requires certain emergency procedures. The doctor who is immediately available does not have privileges to carry out those procedures. The question is whether the doctor has the legal right, and in fact the duty, to carry out the procedures. Does the patient have the right to have that doctor carry out the treatment? There is no hard-and-fast answer.

If that doctor is already treating the patient, the doctor has a duty to carry on in an average, reasonable and prudent manner. This would be to obtain assistance from someone who does have privileges, and to carry on in a reasonable manner until assistance arrives. This may result in the doctor going somewhat beyond the privileges that were granted. However, the doctor must be extremely careful to do this only as is absolutely necessary, to hold off as long as is safe, and to remain within his or her area of competence.

Summary of Principles

1. A patient has a right to go to any licensed physician, dentist or any other health professional who is willing to provide services to that patient.

2. A health professional's right to advertise abilities, expertise and services is severely restricted by the professional regulations governing the particular discipline, therefore limiting the patient's right to this information.

3. A patient's right to choose a doctor may become restricted as governments attempt to control the supply of doctors and where they may practise.

4. A patient does not have a legal right to have a doctor of choice perform any procedure whatsoever in a hospital unless that doctor has been granted the medical staff privileges in that hospital to carry out that procedure.

3

ALTERNATIVE

HEALTH

CARE

The Monopoly of the Medical Establishment

I N MODERN TIMES, Western societies have seen the rise of what can only be described as the medical monopoly. Every province and territory in Canada has an act governing the practice of medicine. In these acts legislators have given doctors a virtual monopoly over the practice of medicine. The right to practise is given exclusively to those who are licensed to practise.

The practice of medicine is defined so broadly that, at least in theory, it includes almost anything that anyone could do to the human body for the purpose of treating or preventing disease or illness. Even surgery that is not related to illness, such as cosmetic surgery, is included. Obstetrics is also included.

The result has been that every few years there is a great debate as to whether certain activities are in fact the practice of medicine. Acupuncture was a prime example when Westerners "discovered" it in China. If it was to be the practice of medicine, the result would be that only physicians could practise it, even if they knew nothing about it. Anyone else, regardless of how knowledgeable or how well trained, would be committing an offence and could be prosecuted.

Over the years it became obvious that dozens of disciplines were carrying out activities that clearly fell within the practice of medicine as it was defined in law. There were traditional professions such as nursing and dentistry, plus the more modern professions of psychology and physiotherapy. Gradually, many others emerged, often being developed from a technical discipline. For example, the respiratory technician gave birth to the respiratory technologist, who became the respiratory therapist. This took place as knowledge in a narrow area was acquired and developed into a specialty that was considered different from that of medicine.

The result was that the medical acts had to make provision for numerous exceptions. These exceptions were either contained in the acts as a statement that the acts did not interfere with the practice of dentistry, for example, or in separate acts giving a similar monopoly to other professions.

However, there are also a growing number of occupations that operate quite openly but are not specifically permitted under any legislation. The practical solution is that the various "monopolies" such as medicine and nursing agree to "allow" these other disciplines to function in what really falls within the monopoly. These so-called subsidiary disciplines or allied health professions really operate at the pleasure of the so-called senior professions.

All of this often occurs without public involvement. The decisions are made by the professions themselves, not by governments. If governments were involved, there might be a far more liberal approach simply because under the health insurance system it would be cheaper for example, to have nurses perform all basic care of patients, rather than family physicians.

The other reality is that for practical reasons "new" disciplines spring up without legislation and are not stopped or cannot be. For example, before there was legislation in Nova Scotia allowing for chiropractors, chiropractors did in fact practise. Their practice was clearly a violation of the provincial medical legislation. It fell within the definition of the practice of medicine but was not carried out by a licensed physician.

Despite this obvious violation of legislation meant to protect the public, no prosecution was launched. The reason was not legal but purely political. Professional legislation is supposed to be public legislation. However, the practice in Canada is that if there is a violation, the public authorities do not prosecute. The attitude of government is that the professions under special acts of the legislature are self-governing and have the responsibility to make certain that their acts are enforced. Therefore, if someone is practising dentistry without a licence, it is up to the provincial dental licensing body — which is not part of government — to launch a prosecution.

This may be fine in theory, but the fact is that prosecuting is an expensive business, like most legal actions. If a long trial is required, and an appeal is launched, the cost is monumental. That must be paid for by the licensing authority, which gets its funds solely from the fees it charges to those who are licensed. The funds do not come out of the public purse, even though the licensing body has the authority to carry out a public function.

In the larger provinces, licensing authorities have the funds and the staff to investigate and prosecute, though sometimes within strained resources. In small provinces, however, many licensing bodies are operated solely by volunteers or part-time staff. They do not have, nor will they ever have, the resources to prosecute those who violate their acts. This means that, at least in theory, the public is left totally unprotected. Anyone could violate a professional act and not be prosecuted, because no one has the money to prosecute and government refuses.

It became immediately obvious that other professionals who work with the human body would not be allowed to practise legally unless some accommodation was made.

The Right to a Non-Physician

The result of all of this is that the patient has the right to get medical or medically related services only from someone who is licensed to provide those services. The theory is that the patient is being protected, since a person who is licensed has met certain basic educational standards that will result in a minimum standard or care for the patient.

This does not mean that people who are not licensed are not competent. It means that their competence has not been recognized. It may not have been recognized because they have not met the specified educational requirements or have not passed the required examinations.

Physicians who come from other countries are not permitted to practise medicine in Canada without taking additional training, even if that training is a repeat of what they took in their own countries. Physicians from the United States, however, are recognized because of the close cooperation and mutual recognition of all Canadian and American medical schools.

The effect on the patient is that a doctor from a non-recognized country or training program is not available, regardless of that doctor's expertise, unless that doctor goes through training recognized by Canada.

The question is whether this is simply a matter of snobbishness. Are Canadian standards higher than those anywhere else in the world, and is that why foreigners are not recognized? Or is it a matter of there being no practical way for Canadian licensing bodies to determine whether Canadian standards are met? There may be a problem comparing examinations in another system and in another language, or in comparing training programs. In some countries there is little uniformity among medical schools, which means that each school and training program would have to be individually assessed. It would be impractical for Canada to assess them.

There is always the suspicion that the reason is economic: it is simply an attempt to keep foreigners, and therefore competition, out. To a certain extent this is true. Since Canada is said to have a surplus of physicians, importing outsiders would overload the system, further straining the already burdened medicare budget.

The result is that patients do not have the right to choose anyone they want to provide their health care since only licensed or otherwise permitted health care providers are available.

This issue has arisen in a number of provinces with respect to midwifery. This profession, which specializes in the delivery of babies, is recognized and practised in most countries. Traditionally Canada has been one of those exceptions where only physicians were permitted to deliver babies.

Many women would prefer a midwife either in hospital or at home, unless there is a complication, in which case a physician would become involved. Because the delivery of babies falls within the definition of the practice of medicine, and only licensed doctors can practise medicine, unless a specific exception is made, midwifery has been illegal in Canada. Only very recently have some provinces legalized it by making it an exception to the monopoly on the practice of medicine given to physicians. In this way midwifery is slowly joining the growing number of health disciplines that have been given special legislation carving out a piece of medicine and allowing them to practise within the scope of that piece. This legislation allowing certain professions to share a piece of medicine with the medical profession has in effect expanded the rights of patients to avail themselves of services.

The approach in Canada, then, has been patronizing in the sense that legislators have felt a need to protect the public. The public could obtain health services only from people who had been licensed to provide those services. The traditional attitude in Canada has been that the public is not in a position to judge whether a health care provider meets certain basic educational and conditional standards. The law has been set up to prevent those who have not met these standards from practising, and therefore has prevented patients from having the right to go to them.

The alternative approach has by and large been rejected in Canada, at least among self-employed health disciplines. This approach would allow any person to practise any profession they wish. What they cannot do is say that they are registered or licensed if they are not. Certain educational criteria would be necessary to be registered or licensed. The effect of such a system would be that the public can decide whether to go to an officially registered person or to someone else. The law would not prevent people from going to unregistered providers. The unregistered providers may be just as good as or even better than those who are registered but do not fulfil the requirements established by the registering authority, or for one reason or another choose not to become registered.

Until fairly recently, most nursing legislation was of this "registration" type. Anyone could practise nursing even if they were not registered. They may have finished their education and graduated but did not want to pay the annual registration fee. As a result, they referred to themselves as graduate nurses rather than as registered nurses. They were hired by hospitals on the same basis as registered nurses.

The move throughout the country, however, has been to make nursing fit the medical model. Under this model, the practice of nursing is protected, rather than only the title "registered nurse." Under the new approach it is no longer possible for hospitals or others to hire those who are not registered to do the work of a registered nurse. This move restricts the freedom of a patient who is hiring a private nurse: the patient cannot hire a person to do the work of a registered nurse unless that person *is* a registered nurse. The problem remains in defining the practice of nursing or the work of a registered nurse. Much of this work can probably be done by a nursing assistant, nurse's aide or licensed practical nurse, depending on the terminology used in each province.

A further possibility that is largely unexplored in Canada is whether a nurse can set up a private practice. Any restriction on such a practice is also a restriction on a patient who may wish to go directly to a nurse rather than to a doctor. A nurse can be hired for private duty in a home or hospital. What we are not used to in Canada is a nurse who has a private office.

Essentially, there is nothing illegal in this. The question concerns the scope of such practice. If it is clearly within the scope of nursing, there is no problem. If, however, it slides over the the practice of medicine, it could be an offence under the medical act of the province.

Nursing practice begins to slip into the practice of medicine if it is shown that a nurse has made a diagnosis, traditionally the exclusive field of the physician. The reality is that nurses routinely tell patients "what is wrong" and whether the services of a doctor are needed. Whether this is the act of diagnosing remains undecided.

There is no clear answer, though the financial restraints and the general trend in the delivery to health care will undoubtedly expand the practice of nursing to allow this type of arrangement. As this happens, the patient will have increasingly greater rights to have primary access to a nurse rather than to a physician. The difficulty is that if such a practice is universally adopted, the Canadian medicare system might require that primary access take place through a nurse. Many health problems could then be solved at a much lower cost without the intervention of a physician. Nurses could become the "gatekeepers" of the system. From a patient's rights point of view, what would at first be an expansion of the patient's right to have direct access to a nurse rather than to a doctor would in fact result in a restriction.

Because Canada is a federation of jurisdictions and because the governance of the professions is provincial rather than federal, certain disciplines are available in one province but not in another. Also, a member of one discipline may be licensed to practise in one province but not elsewhere. Although this may be regarded as a matter of the rights of the member of that profession, it does limit patient rights as well. It means that a patient does not have the right to have someone from another province provide treatment unless that provider is legally permitted to do so in the province where the treatment is to take place. However, the patient is free to travel to where the provider is permitted to practice.

The Right to Unorthodox Treatments

Many patients find themselves in a situation in which treatments given by their doctors do not work. They, and sometimes their doctors, seek alternative care, but still under the supervision of a physician.

There is no doubt that experimental and even unorthodox treatments can be attempted. The law lays down three restrictions, however.

The first is that the patient must give a fully informed consent. (See chapter 4, "Consent to Treatment.") Unlike consent to ordinary treatment and care, the law imposes a much heavier burden on physicians when unusual treatments are proposed. This burden is in the area of how much the patient must be told. Ordinarily, the patient must be told of all risks that the *average patient* would want to know. When the treatment is unusual or experimental, the patient is entitled to know even more, even about those risks that may not ordinarily be considered serious. The law has not spelled out what that includes, but it certainly includes a great deal more information about the potential risks and benefits, along with the unusual nature of the treatment. The patient is entitled to a full explanation of the alternatives, including a comparison of the proposed treatment with the usual treatment.

The second legal restriction is that the patient is entitled, as in any treatment, to receive average, reasonable and prudent care. (See chapter 5, "Negligence and Standards of Care.") Since the unusual treatment may carry unusual risks, the doctor has the duty to take whatever precautions are necessary to at least minimize those risks. Because the treatment is unusual, the law requires the doctor to abide by a higher standard of care in treating the patient than would be otherwise be the case. Any injury that results from the failure to meet this higher standard and is reasonably foreseeable would be considered the result of negligence, and the patient would be entitled to compensation. The problem is in proving what this higher standard should be.

The third restriction on unconventional treatment arises from the medical disciplinary body of the province. In some cases, that body has found that a treatment is so unusual that it is simply not professional to use it. The doctor could be disciplined and even barred from the practice of medicine — even though the patient consented to the treatment. The patient therefore has no legal right to treatment that the medical disciplinary authority has decided is unprofessional conduct.

A similar restriction arises if the proposed treatment is so unusual and even dangerous that it falls within section 219 of the Criminal Code of Canada, which defines criminal negligence. Section 221 makes causing bodily harm to a person by criminal negligence a criminal offence. The maximum penalty is ten years' imprisonment. Section 220 makes death by criminal negligence a criminal offence with a maximum penalty of life imprisonment.

The Code requires the accused to have shown "wanton or reckless disregard for the lives or safety of other persons." The doctor does not have to be intentionally negligent. Being indifferent to the patient's safety is enough to be guilty of this offence.

The Criminal Code imposes an additional duty on the doctor, under section 216. This section requires anyone who undertakes surgical or medical treatment, except in cases of necessity, to have and to use reasonable knowledge, skill and care. A doctor who administers a treatment that is not considered normal or reasonable by the medical profession may well be considered in breach of this section. As with the other restrictions, the patient does not have a legal right to remove any criminal responsibility from the doctor under this section.

New and Unapproved Drugs

The use of drugs by physicians in a way that is unusual falls within all of the restrictions outlined above. Prescribing drugs, or even recommending drugs that do not require a prescription, is considered treatment. All the restrictions of any treatment and the effect on a patient's rights apply.

In addition, drugs in Canada are controlled under two federal acts, the Food and Drugs Act and the Narcotic Control Act. Both are designed to regulate the public substances that may affect health or life and thereby restrict the right of the patient to drugs (and treatment) that do not conform with these acts.

The Food and Drugs Act, and the regulations made under it, deals with food, drugs, cosmetics and therapeutic devices. A patient who wants a certain drug, even if it is recommended by a physician, has no legal right to that drug unless it conforms with the legislation and has been approved by Health and Welfare Canada. It is possible, however, that with special dispensation from the federal authorities a drug that has not been authorized for sale in Canada may be allowed for a patient.

Treatments Abroad

Every so often the press covers the story of a patient who goes to another country to obtain treatment that is not available in Canada. In some cases the treatment is not available because no Canadian physician will perform it. Either there is general agreement that the treatment does not meet appropriate standards or physicians disapprove of it. In other instances, physicians know nothing about it and are therefore unwilling to try it.

Even if a physician is willing to attempt certain procedures that are unusual in Canada, Canadian hospitals may not permit it. A hospital may not be able to provide the appropriate support for the procedure or because of the general disapproval of it in the health field.

The fact that certain procedures may be available in other countries does not give a patient a legal right to have the same or similar procedures in Canada. Similarly, a Canadian patient who goes abroad for a procedure does not carry along Canadian legal rights. The law of consent, duty of care and any other matter will be the law of the foreign country. Even if a lawsuit was launched by the patient against the foreign providers of care in a Canadian court, the court would have to apply the law of the foreign country. In addition, any judgement obtained would have to be enforced in that country.

The principle is that people who travel are subject to the law of wherever they happen to be at the time. They do not take the law of their home country with them. Even when travelling within Canada, a patient is subject to the laws of the province or territory where that person happens to be at the time, not where the patient lives.

Summary of Principles
1. Provincial law gives the medical profession a monopoly on the practice of medicine, which is defined so broadly that it includes almost all care and treatment of human ailments.
2. Numerous other health disciplines have been permitted either by legislation or by agreement of the medical licensing authorities to carry out certain practices that might otherwise be considered the practice of medicine. Among these are nursing, dentistry, physiotherapy and psychology.
3. Patients do not have the legal right to obtain health services from someone who is not licensed or otherwise permitted to provide those services regardless of that person's training or competency, and regardless of whether that person is a member of what is a recognized health profession.

4. A patient does not have the right to a treatment or procedure that in Canada is regarded as unprofessional, beneath accepted Canadian standards or otherwise illegal.

5. A patient in Canada does not have the right to a procedure in Canada that is permitted in another country but not permitted in Canada.

6. A Canadian patient who obtains alternative health care in another country is subject to the law of that country, not the law of Canada.

▼ 4
CONSENT
TO
TREATMENT

OR YEARS THE SUBJECT of consent to treatment has been a hot and controversial topic. At almost every medico-legal conference in the world, the subject is on the agenda, and Canada is no exception. It is the one subject more than almost any other that brings doctors and other health professionals into direct and emotional conflict with lawyers.

Despite the incendiary nature of the issue, the vast majority of malpractice suits brought by patients are not concerned with consent to treatment. They are usually concerned with standard of care.

What happens in a malpractice suit is that the patient is unhappy with the manner in which care or treatment was given or with the result. The allegation or accusation in the suit (drafted by the lawyer, not the patient) is that the doctor, hospital, the nurse, nursing home or whoever the defendant happens to be failed to care for the patient in a manner that met average, reasonable and prudent standards, and as a direct and reasonably foreseeable result, the patient was injured.

The lawyer frequently adds a second allegation: that the patient did not consent to the treatment in the first place. Invariably, however, this cannot be proven.

A third allegation frequently added is that although the patient consented, the consent was not valid, or it was negligently obtained. It is this allegation that causes the most controversy. Despite three Supreme Court of Canada decisions on the matter, there is still confusion over what is necessary to properly obtain a patient's consent.

It is possible to sue a doctor, dentist or other health care provider on the consent issue alone, but that is an infrequent approach. By combining the three allegations, which of course the patient as a plaintiff has to prove to win the case, what is being said is that the defendant was negligent in the treatment, and even if that is not true, the patient did not consent to it, and even if that was not true, the consent was negligently obtained.

Although these issues are settled somewhat differently in different countries, the issues are the same. Why are they so controversial?

The reason arises from the basic mentality of health care providers and that of lawyers. All health disciplines, whether medicine and surgery, nursing, dentistry, physiotherapy or psychology, are trained with the same approach. The view is that the patient has a complaint derived from some malfunction in the body or the mind. It is the job of the health care system to determine what is wrong and to make it right. It is assumed by health professionals that merely by arriving in a health care provider's office or facility, a person consents to having this done. The health care professional determines what the patient needs and responds to those needs.

Lawyers and the law operate on a very different basis. The law is not primarily interested in a person's needs. The law is interested in a person's *wants*. If what the person needs and what the person wants are not the same, frequently the law sides with the person's wants, if there is a right to have those wants fulfilled.

The result of this conflict is that if a person who is sick or dying comes to the attention of a doctor or other health professional but does not want to be treated, the law will support that desire. This places health professionals in a terribly quandary. They are trained to *do some-*

thing, to respond to the needs of that person. They have also taken a professional oath to respond to the needs of those who are suffering. However, it is the decision of the patient that is paramount, based on the fundamental principle of law, the right to bodily freedom.

It is this basic principle that brings law and health care into conflict. On the legal side, every person has the right to decide who shall touch or otherwise interfere with their body and what that touching will be. The legal and ethical duties of health professionals are always subject to the rights of the patients, unless those rights have been specifically removed by the law. This means that every person has the right to refuse medical care regardless of whether they need it and regardless of how foolish that decision might be.

On the medical side, there is a basic assumption that everyone has an interest in having his or her health needs fulfilled, and that it is inconceivable that anyone would not want their needs looked after. A person who refuses treatment places the health care professionals in a most frustrating position, since their professional role is to determine needs and care for those needs. Health professionals have an intense desire to treat a patient, whether or not the patient wants to be treated. It is a matter of priorities. Is the health of a human being the ultimate social value, or is it the right of a human being to remain untouched regardless of the consequences to health or life? Society protects the right to remain untouched, despite the frustration of the health care providers.

There are a number of exceptions to the rule. The exceptions, however, are very narrowly interpreted by the courts, since the basic right over one's body and the freedom to remain untouched by others is not given away lightly.

The Myths of Consent to Treatment

Consent to treatment is the first major exception to the rule that a person is not to be touched by others. It is the authority given by the patient that allows physicians, dentists, nurses, physiotherapists or others to interfere with the patient's body.

1. *The consent form is consent.* On entering hospital as an in-patient (that is, for an overnight stay) and for many out-patient procedures,

hospitals require patients to sign a "consent to treatment" form. Many hospital administrators, doctors and staff believe that this form constitutes consent to treatment. Patients also believe that it is their consent to treatment. In fact, this is not true.

The consent to treatment form frequently consists of a statement such as "I hereby consent to _____, the nature, risks, benefits and reasonable alternatives of which have been explained to me by Dr. _____." To see that this is not consent, one needs to know what is meant by consent.

Consent may be defined as an agreement by a patient to allow a particular person or group of persons to perform certain invasions of his or her body. To do this, the patient has to know what is going to be done. A medical term placed in the blank tells the patient nothing unless it has been explained so the patient understands. This may have been done, but the explanation is not on the form.

The patient must also be legally and mentally competent to consent to treatment. The consent must be voluntary. An involuntary consent is not consent at all. As we shall see, the most controversial of all the criteria necessary for a valid consent is that the patient must be "informed" of the nature, risks, benefits and reasonable alternatives of the procedure.

If these criteria have not been fulfilled, the signing of a form stating that the patient has consented is meaningless. The real purpose of the consent form is that if there is a lawsuit alleging that consent did not take place, the hospital will be able to produce a signed paper showing that it did. However, the court will then examine the facts of what happened before the signing, which may very well show that the form is evidence of nothing except that the patient signed something.

2. *The doctor knows best.* There is a belief among patients and doctors that "the doctor knows best" and that, therefore, the patient really does not have a choice. Patients will frequently say that they "had to" have the operation, or "They put me in hospital."

While it is true that the doctor may know more than the patient about the patient's body, it is not true that the doctor or anyone else knows what is best for the patient. Only the patient can determine that, based on professional advice provided by physicians and others, and on the patient's assessment of what is best given the patient's understanding of his or her own feelings about the medical situation at hand. No one can determine what is best for someone else. Even if the decision is irresponsible for one person, it may not be for another.

3. *Do not upset the patient.* Many physicians take the attitude that if the patient was told the nature of the procedure and particularly the risks, the patient would be upset. This in turn could affect the patient's ability to withstand the procedure or could even cause complications. The argument is also given that the patient might be so upset that consent to a required procedure would be unreasonably refused, and the patient would suffer as a result.

This position is understandable only in the context of the physician taking the role of protector of the patient's well-being, and not simply to provide services that are required and *desired*. This protector approach has to a large extent fallen out of favour, at least with much of the population.

First of all, it is highly questionable that the patient would be so upset that undesirable medical complications would ensue. Even if this were so, the current view is that the desire to not upset the patient does not take priority over the patient's legal right to information about what is going to be done to his or her body, to accept the risks and to make the decision whether to have the procedure performed.

One wondered whether the motivation for not informing the patient is not so much to protect the patient from emotional trauma as to avoid having to explain the intricacies of the procedure to the patient or having to deal with the emotional reaction that might arise.

Furthermore, it is the doctor's job to inform the patient in a manner that will at least enable the patient to control any reaction and to rationally make an informed decision. This is also true with respect to surgical risks that are infrequent but do occur, such as anaesthetic deaths. Putting these risks in the appropriate perspective for the patient and balancing those risks with the risks of not having the surgery is part of the doctor's role. The essential difficulty seems to be that many medical practitioners, like many specialists in other professions, including law, do not see education as a basic part of their role. For many doctors, teaching a patient is an interference in their role to "fix" things, rather than part of the practice of medicine.

4. *A visit to the doctor is consent.* Many physicians and even some patients believe that when a patient consults a doctor for advice, that is in itself consent to the treatment that is proposed. This is not true. The patient goes to a doctor for advice. The doctor, on the basis of the patient's history and subsequent examinations and tests, advises what should be done. Only then does the patient decide whether to consent. Until then, the patient has not yet given up the right to remain untouched.

5. *A husband consents for his wife.* At one time an unmarried woman was under the protection of her father. When she got married she was given to her husband, who assumed this role. Somehow this was translated into medical care, whereby a husband was asked for his consent for his wife's treatment. This practice faded, with the exception of treatment that might affect marital relations, which is taken to include sexual relations and reproductive ability. (See chapters 13, "Abortion," and 14, "Sterilization.") The practice was enshrined in legislation only in Quebec; elsewhere it was followed as a matter of practice. The Quebec law was changed over twenty years ago and eventually it was realized in English Canada that this was no longer the law and should not be the practice. Not only does a woman not need her husband's consent but such consent should not be sought except in cases of emergency when the wife is incapable of consenting. It is irrelevant as to what effect the treatment may have.

Because husbands were never under the "protection" of their wives, it was never necessary to seek the wife's consent for her husband's treatment, even if the procedure might affect the marital relationship.

CRITERIA FOR VALID CONSENT

Criterion #1: How Much to Tell the Patient
Foremost among the criteria necessary to have a valid consent, one that authorizes what otherwise would be an interference with the

patient's right not be touched, is the right of the patient to be "informed." The question is: How much does the doctor have to tell the patient?

Until the 1980s, the rule in Canada was unclear. It was simply that the doctor had a duty to tell the patient what was reasonable to tell the patient. What was "reasonable" depended on the circumstances. This fuzzy rule may have satisfied lawyers and judges, but it certainly did not satisfy doctors. The medical profession was unclear about how much information was deemed reasonable. The lawyers were of little assistance, except to say that if a doctor got sued for not telling the patient enough, the courts would determine whether in fact this was so. This may have been fine for lawyers, but it was not very good for doctors — and not very good for patients. Doctors were never told exactly what to do in order not to get sued. The practice of not telling patients very much therefore continued, and there were few lawsuits based on improper consent to treatment.

In the early 1980s, two cases before the Supreme Court of Canada dealt with exactly this question of how much the patient has a right to be told in order to give a valid consent. In the case of *Hopp v. Lepp* the court said that the patient must be advised of all *material or special risks*. This was taken to mean all serious risks of serious injury or death.

The message that emerged seemed to be that doctors, dentists and other care providers have a duty to tell the patient as much as possible. Although words of this sort fit nicely with the judicial mind, they were utterly confusing to the medical mind: they meant nothing. How serious is serious? For example, every case of general anaesthesia carries with it a risk of death. Does that mean that every patient who is advised to have surgery under a general anaesthetic must be told of the risk of death? If the risk of death is one in a million, must the patient be told? One in one hundred thousand? One in a thousand? One in ten? At what point does the patient no longer have a right to be told, and the doctor no duty to tell?

In the flood of consent cases that have arisen before Canadian courts since this case, it has been easy for the courts to find that the risk of a procedure was material or special and that therefore the patient had a legal right to be told about it before being asked to consent. Despite these findings, however, the patients have been losing most of the cases.

The reason — highly legalistic and confusing — is as follows. Before the first Supreme Court consent case, it was felt that if the criteria necessary for a valid consent were not present or not fulfilled, the consent was invalid. If that was the case, the surgery was equal to a battery, which is almost like a punch in the nose or any other assault by one human being on another. The victim could sue even if there was no injury because the law felt that an unconsented-to assault was such an affront on a human being that the victim should be compensated even if the victim did not suffer any physical injury.

However, a second Supreme Court case, *Reibl v. Hughes*, handed down in the early 1980s, pointed out that in most cases patients do consent to treatment. The problem is that their consent has not been properly obtained because the material or special risks have not been properly explained to them. What therefore has happened, the court said, was that the doctor has been negligent in obtaining the patient's consent.

This was a landmark decision because in suing someone for negligence, it is necessary for the plaintiff to prove that the defendant failed in his or her duty to the plaintiff and as a result the plaintiff suffered injury. This means that a patient who sues a doctor for negligence must prove that the doctor failed in his duty to the patient and the patient was injured. When this rule is placed in the consent context, it is usually easy to prove that the doctor failed in his duty to properly advise the patient about the risks of the procedure. The patient must, however, show that as a result of not being properly informed, he consented to something he would not otherwise have consented to, and as a result suffered the risk and was injured.

If it were simply for the patient to say that if he had been informed he never would have consented, then most of these cases would have been won by patients. However, that is not the rule. The rule handed down by the Supreme Court of Canada is that the patient can say he was injured only if the average person in the patient's position would *not have consented* on being told of the risks. Then the patient, by not being told and consenting, can say that he has been injured.

This rule clearly illustrates how far out of touch judges and lawyers can be from the ordinary affairs of average people and from the practicalities of everyday medical practice. The result is that doctors who fail in their duty to properly advise patients are rarely sued successfully. The courts usually find that if the patient was an average, reasonable person, he would have consented to the procedure (and therefore to the risks) even if he had known all the risks. It does not matter what the actual patient now says he would have done if he had known of the risks beforehand.

This rule not only puts patients in a difficult position when their right to be informed of the risks has been denied without them knowing it, it also presents doctors and other health care providers with a dilemma. It is hardly realistic, or fair, to ask a doctor to determine what an average person would have done if he had been in the patient's position and and had been informed of the risks. Doctors simply do not think along those lines. They think of what a patient needs, and how to fulfil those needs.

The judges also have sent contradictory messages to the medical and health professions. On one hand, they have said, "Tell the patient as much as possible so that the patient can make a reasonably informed decision." On the other hand, the court has said that "if you do not, do not worry about it, because it will be difficult to successfully sue you."

One example of how consent cases are handled in Canada is the 1985 Ontario case of *Ferguson v. Hamilton Civic Hospitals*, in which 58-year-old William Ferguson underwent an angiogram to diagnose an eye problem. He had been warned of the risk of death from the procedure but not of the risk of stroke. Although there was no negligence in carrying out the procedure, Mr. Ferguson did have a stroke and was left a quadriplegic. The court did note that he had not been properly informed, but since a reasonable patient in Mr. Ferguson's position would have consented even if he had been informed of the risk of stroke, Mr. Ferguson could not complain that he had not been informed. The issue went to appeal, and the Ontario Court of Appeal upheld the decision. Before the appeal decision was handed down, Mr. Ferguson died.

There are cases in which the patients have won. The 1987 Saskatchewan Court of Appeal case of *Haughian v. Paine* dealt with

55-year-old Patrick Haughian, who sued neurosurgeon Dr. Kenneth Paine, who had performed surgery on Mr. Haughian to correct a herniated disc. In obtaining the patient's consent, no mention was made of any risk of total paralysis or death. The plaintiff was paralysed after the surgery. While this condition was largely corrected, he was still left disabled. In the court's view, that the risk was estimated at less than one in five hundred did not remove the duty of the doctor to tell the patient of the risk. The court concluded that if there had been full disclosure of the risks, the patient would not have consented.

The patient is not entitled to a full scientific lecture on the nature, risks, benefits and reasonable alternatives, unless the patient asks. It is not clear, however, just how much the patient *is* entitled to. Whatever it is, the patient is entitled to have questions answered and to be informed in a way he or she can understand. Signing a consent to treatment form does not do this.

The real problem for doctors is the patient who refuses to be informed but says, "I trust you, Doctor." This may not protect the doctor who does not warn of the risks.

The key to the solution is for patients to ask questions about risks, benefits and alternatives. They should also ask about the risks and benefits of the alternatives, remembering that one alternative that must always be considered is to do nothing.

Exceptions to the Rule

As with almost everything in law, and perhaps in life, there are always exceptions. There is an exception to the rule that the patient must be adequately informed. It is usually referred to as the therapeutic privilege. The courts have recognized that there may be some circumstances in which giving the patient information would interfere with the treatment. However, this possibility is very limited. It cannot be used as an excuse to keep the patient in ignorance because of the possibility of upsetting the patient. An example of where it might be applied would be in psychiatric cases in which a placebo or a non-active drug is given so that the patient thinks that a drug is taken and reacts accordingly. Informing the patient of this would destroy the basis of the treatment.

Another exception to the rule is that information may be withheld when it is not practical to fully advise the patient. For example, if the patient was in an emergency situation but was mentally competent, and the time spent to fully inform the patient would endanger the patient's life or health, the treatment should proceed without the patient receiving the complete information.

The major exception, however, is that of the medico-legal emergency. Such a situation requires the patient to be lacking in the mental capacity to understand the information that the doctor must provide. The patient may be unconscious, or in a state of shock, or under the influence of alcohol or drugs. Ordinarily in those situations, treatment should be delayed until the patient is mentally capable of understanding the information and either consenting or refusing. However, if mental capability is lacking and any delay in treatment would endanger the patient's life or health, the law assumes that the patient would consent if mental capacity was present. Therefore, it is not necessary to advise the patient or to even seek consent.

The important point to remember in this exception is that it is not enough to have a medical emergency. The patient must also be mentally incapable of understanding the information necessary to give a valid consent.

A further exception to the rule requiring consent to treatment exists when legislation allows for involuntary treatment. If all the criteria of the legislation are met, treatment may take place without informing the patient and without any consent being obtained. Legislation of this sort establishes a specific procedure that must be followed before treatment can be given. If the criteria or the procedure is not met, any treatment given without the patient's consent or against the patient's will is strictly illegal and may be considered by the courts as assault and battery, for which the patient may be compensated. This exception applies in the areas of mental illness (but not all mental illness) and in communicable disease (but not all communicable diseases).

Criterion #2: Consent Must be Voluntary
A basic principle in the law of consent is that the patient cannot be forced to consent, nor placed under such compulsion or duress that

consent is not a voluntary act. Any fraud or misrepresentation that causes the patient to consent will destroy the validity of consent.

This requirement creates the problem of what is meant by voluntary. Is any consent truly voluntary? Most patients do not want to be treated. They accept treatment to achieve a cure, or to avoid pain, disability or death. Can a patient who says "What choice have I?" really be acting voluntarily?

However, if a patient can indeed choose between treatment or no treatment, the law regards the consent as voluntary.

Criterion #3: Mental Capability

To give a valid consent, a person must have the mental capability to do so. This does not mean that the person must be mentally competent or unimpaired. It means that the patient must have the mental capability of understanding that he or she has the right to refuse treatment, and can understand the information given regarding the nature, risks, benefits and alternatives to the treatment.

Therefore, if a person is mentally ill, under the influence of drugs or alcohol, or mentally retarded, it does not necessarily mean that consent cannot be given. (See chapter 18, "Mental Illness.") Even under these circumstances, a person may have the mental capability of being able to consent to treatment. Depending on the type or complexity of treatment, it is possible that a person may have the mental capability of consenting to one treatment but not to another.

In the case of mental illness, it may be possible for a person to have the mental capability one day but not another. It is also possible for a person to be mentally capable of carrying out certain acts, such as committing a crime or entering into a contract, but not mentally capable of consenting to treatment. A patient may be able to consent to treatment on one part of the body but not on another because of mental illness that affects the patient's attitudes towards one part of the body.

Criterion #4: Legal Capacity

As a general rule, everyone has the legal capacity to consent to treatment or to refuse treatment. The only exception is when that capacity has been specifically taken away by legislation. This applies in cases that fall under mental health legislation. A person who suffers from a mental disorder and is dangerous to himself or others may be placed in a psychiatric hospital without consent. The same applies under communicable disease legislation.

A person's legal capacity to consent or refuse can also be removed by the courts if it is found that the person lacks the mental capacity to consent. A guardian is then appointed to act for such a person. Various hospital acts have similar provisions.

Such enactments come into effect, however, only if the procedure outlined in them is followed exactly. If it is not, the person still maintains the legal capacity to consent or refuse.

Criterion #5: Consent to Treatment Actually Performed

When a person consents to a particular procedure and another procedure is performed, the consent is not valid, and the patient could sue for assault and battery. This may easily happen in dentistry, when a patient consents to the extraction of one tooth and several are removed. It may also happen in surgery, when a patient has consented to surgery on a particular organ and an additional organ is removed. If this removal is an emergency in which there is an immediate threat to the life or health of the patient, the courts may allow it. However, if the removal of the second organ could have waited, it must. From a medical point of view it is certainly better to perform the second procedure without scheduling a second operation. Yet the patient has the right to be consulted about the second procedure and decide whether to have it done. To avoid these problems, hospitals frequently seek the consent of a patient to procedures that may take place once the operation is in progress. However, asking a patient to consent to a particular procedure and, vaguely, "such other procedures as may be deemed necessary" is probably ineffective. The patient generally has no idea what he or she is consenting to.

Criterion #6: Consent to the Person Doing the Procedure

Until recently it was theoretically true that if a patient consented to a particular surgeon to do an operation, any other surgeon who performed the procedure would be committing a battery against the patient, for which the patient could be compensated, even if the surgery was well done. The Quebec Superior Court, in the 1992 decision of *Currie v. Blundell*, made it clear that a surgeon could not delegate an important part of an operation to another surgeon for whom the patient had not consented. At least in that case, the patient had the right to demand that the surgeon who was retained actually perform the operation.

This case will not necessarily be followed in other provinces, or in other circumstances, but it is an indication that the courts are not favourably disposed to hospitals and doctors playing "bait and switch." To get around this problem, most hospitals ask patients to consent to procedures being performed by particular doctors with the assistance of various others. This does not prevent a patient from insisting on a particular doctor only. And that doctor will not necessarily agree to such a request.

Can Someone Other Than the Patient Give Consent?

Ordinarily, if a patient is not mentally capable of consenting to treatment and a court has not appointed a guardian to act on the patient's behalf, hospitals will seek the consent of the spouse or an adult child or sibling who seems to be looking after the patient's affairs. Often there was no legal authority for this, but it has been the accepted practice. In some provinces, legislation specifically allows for this. If there is no time to obtain consent because of an emergency, the law permits treatment without consent.

The difficulty facing health institutions is that of a disagreement among family members. A further problem arises when a person who is clearly looking after the patient's affairs has no formal relationship with the patient, such as a friend.

This situation also creates problems for patients, since it means that those who make the medical decisions may not be those whom the patient would want. To avoid this situation, an increasing number of provinces are enacting what are known as durable powers of attorney legislation. This type of legislation specifically allows one person to appoint another to make medical decisions if the person becomes mentally incapable of doing so.

The problem with this legislation is that it often has certain restrictions or the document must be written in a particular manner. If the legislation is not followed exactly, the document may not be valid, and the person appointed cannot act. It is therefore advisable to have a lawyer draft the document. It should also be carried on one's person at all times, since if no one can find the document when a treatment decision has to be made, the hospital will have to assume that it does not exist.

The Effect of Legislation

The traditional legal approach to consent to treatment was based on court decisions. This meant that many issues raised by people in the health field had never been dealt with by the courts. One could only speculate as to what the courts might do if they had to decide on a particular issue. While this provided some uncertainty, it also provided flexibility. In fact, in the past few years there have been a sufficient number of consent cases before the courts that the issues are not nearly as uncertain as they were fifteen years ago.

Despite this trend, many governments are determined to pass laws on the subject of consent — although it has been suggested that such legislation will only cause further lawsuits as parties squabble over the meaning of the legislation. As well, much of the material in these acts is already law as handed down by the courts. The courts are in a position to mould the law as time goes on, whereas in legislation, changes to who can consent and how consent is given will have to take place through political lobbying. The effect is to turn a matter of personal relationships and the legal standards affecting them into a highly political, bureaucratic and static contract.

Several provinces have dabbled in the area of consent, particularly in mental health legislation. The Consent to Treatment Act in Ontario is the most extensive in the country; it outlines the elements of consent and what a patient must be told to be "informed" and stipulates that consent may be expressed or implied and that it may be withdrawn at any time. It deals with the patient's capacity to consent, who can give a substitute consent and the role of a guardian. It also outlines recourse to the provincial advocacy service and sets out an appeal mechanism for decisions made for patients who are found incapable of consenting.

In determining patient's rights, it is therefore essential to examine the appropriate provincial consent legislation in detail. If the legislation does not provide answers for the situation at hand, it will be necessary to draw inferences from the legislation or to fall back on common law to fill in the gaps in the English provinces, and the Civil Law in Quebec.

Advance Directives

What are commonly known as advance directives have in the past been restricted to "living wills." (See chapter 23, "Dying and Death.") An advance directive, though, covers situations far broader than that of death. It is a document that outlines a person's refusal to consent to certain treatments or types of care in the future if that person is mentally unable to express either consent or refusal.

The question is often raised whether it is necessary to have legislation to allow for an advance directive. The idea of refusing treatment in advance, when at the time of the refusal the treatment was not even necessary, proposed or thought of, has bothered many. The problem has been that until one is facing a situation in which treatment is proposed, one cannot be adequately informed of the consequences of refusal, since the circumstances surrounding the treatment are unknown in advance, and it is those circumstances that would govern the risks of which the patient has a right to be informed.

Despite these doubts, the courts have now made it clear, in the 1987 Ontario Court of Appeal decision *Malette v. Shulman*, that a person can refuse treatment in advance without legislation to allow it. However, governments may be moving towards legislating. Where legislation exists, patients will have to follow it, and it will outline how the directive is to be written.

The *Malette v. Shulman* case involved a Jehovah's Witness who carried a card stating that regardless of the circumstances she was never to be given blood or blood products because of her religious beliefs. She was involved in a car accident and was taken to hospital unconscious. The attending physician was informed of the card and her beliefs but gave her blood transfusions regardless. He felt that without blood she would die. She survived, and subsequently sued the doctor.

There is no doubt that the doctor acted in the interest of saving her life. He also felt that it would be unethical for him to do nothing and allow her to die. The court rejected his arguments. Mrs. Malette had the legal right to determine what she wanted to do with her body. She had the legal right to choose which treatment, if any, she desired. No doctor could impose his professional ethics on a patient. The court made it clear that a doctor acting in the "best interests" of the patient is bound by the right of the patient over his or her body. Best interests do not necessarily equal medical needs.

Withdrawal of Consent
It has always been understood that a patient who had given consent could withdraw that consent, in which case the procedure could not go ahead. A recent problem, however, was presented to the Supreme Court of Canada in the Ontario case of *Ciarlariello v. Schacter*. In the middle of an angiogram, Mrs. Ciarlariello began moaning and yelling. Her breathing became rapid and she flexed her legs. She could not respond to the doctor's questions. When she calmed down, she said, "Enough, no more, stop the test."

The test was stopped. She then asked that it be continued. The final injection was administered, but the patient had a rare reaction, which rendered her a quadriplegic. She later died.

Mr. Justice Peter Cory of Canada's highest court made it very clear when he said, "If, during the course of a medical procedure, a patient withdraws the consent to that procedure, then the doctors must halt the process. This duty to stop does no more than recognize every individual's basic right to make decisions concerning his or her own body."

The second question before the court was whether it was necessary to inform the patient once again before continuing. The Ontario Court of Appeal had said that this was up to the doctor. Absolutely not, said the Supreme Court of Canada. It is up to the patient. However, Justice Cory pointed out that one must look at what the patient would like to know concerning the continuation. He said that if there had been any significant change in the risks involved or if the need for the continuation had changed, the patient would have the legal right to be informed of this additional information. If there had been no change in the circumstances, then it would not be necessary to advise the patient of the same information that had been given originally. The court's conclusion was that the patient is entitled to have any information pertaining to any changes in the circumstances in order to decide whether to continue.

Once again, the law is absolutely clear. It is the patient who decides whether a recommended procedure is to be performed, not the doctor.

Summary of Principles

1. Every person has a fundamental right to be free of other people interfering with his or her body without consent.
2. Every person has the right to refuse medical or other treatment, even when that treatment or care is required.
3. Consent is a process in which a person voluntarily agrees to be treated after being given sufficient information on which to base a decision either to be treated or to not be treated.
4. The patient has the right to receive sufficient information to make a decision regarding treatment, including information on the nature, risks, benefits and reasonable alternatives of having or not having the proposed treatment.
5. The patient has the right to receive information on all the material or special risks of serious injury or death of the proposed treatment or procedure even if the possibility of it occurring is small.
6. Consent to treatment is not given by merely signing a form.
7. The decision to receive treatment or to refuse treatment is made by the patient, not by the doctor, whose role is to recommend and give advice.
8. The patient's consent cannot be implied from a visit to a doctor; it must be specific to the treatment proposed.
9. A wife does not need her husband's consent, regardless of the proposed procedure.
10. If a person is mentally incapable of consenting and care is urgently required to protect health or life, treatment can take place without consent, though close family members or a spouse usually consent on behalf of the patient.

11. Provincial legislation has taken away the right to refuse treatment in the case of some communicable diseases and mental illness when the person is dangerous to himself or others.

12. A person who is mentally ill or retarded can consent if that person can understand what it means to consent and can understand the information given.

13. A person can lose the legal right to consent if a court appoints a guardian to consent on that person's behalf.

14. The patient has the right to consent specifically to the proposed procedure and any extensions to which the patient agrees.

15. The patient has the right to consent to have a specific person or group of persons perform the procedure.

16. If a patient is not mentally capable of consenting, a spouse or family member may give a substitute consent according to the provisions of provincial legislation or any prior designation made by the patient if such a designation is permitted by provincial legislation.

5

NEGLIGENCE

AND

STANDARDS

OF CARE

W HEN A HEALTH CARE PROFESSIONAL OR FACILITY — doctor, dentist, hospital, nursing home or any other person or institution — is sued, the suit is invariably for negligence. The word *negligence*, however, is often confused with the word *malpractice*.

Malpractice, or bad practice, is a much broader term and one that is not very precise. It includes all actions brought by a patient against a health professional or facility arising out of the provision of health care. It may be negligence, and usually is. It could also be assault or battery, if the accusation is that treatment was given without consent. It could also be false imprisonment if a patient alleges that he was confined in a hospital against his will.

What is Negligence?
People often use the word *negligence* to mean sloppy work, or work not meeting certain standards. Although sloppy or substandard work

may be negligent, it is not necessarily so. A person may be sloppy or substandard but not negligent. The person may even cause injury but not be negligent. Negligence is a legal term that has a precise and often technical meaning. As a result, it is difficult and expensive for a patient to prove that a doctor, nurse, therapist or technologist has been negligent.

The concept of negligence is important because it is based on one of the most important of all patient's rights, the right to receive a reasonable standard of care. Once a person becomes a patient of a health care professional, agency or facility, that health care provider has a legal duty to carry out the care according to this standard. This right applies after the patient consents to receiving the care or treatment.

Negligence is the failure of the health professional, agency or facility to give the patient that right. Negligence is therefore the negative side of a positive legal right. In other words, it is the failure to get the standard of care to which the patient has a legal right.

Negligence can be defined as the failure to receive average, reasonable and prudent standards of care *and* as a reasonably foreseeable result suffer injury. The client of an architect, accountant, lawyer, plumber or electrician has the same right, and can sue for negligence.

The concept of negligence can be described in the following diagram:

negligence
=

| 1) the failure |
| 2) to meet average, reasonable and prudent standards |
| 3) in the circumstances |

+

| 4) reasonably foreseeable injury (or death) |

The Consequences of the Definition

Applying this definition to a negligence lawsuit brought by a patient against a health care provider raises a number of factors that make it difficult to win the suit.

1. There is an assumption in the law that the right of the patient to receive care or treatment according to the average, reasonable and prudent standard was fulfilled. As a result, if a patient sues on the basis that this did not happen, the burden is on the patient to prove his or her case, not on the defendant to prove that the patient is wrong. This means that it is the patient (the plaintiff in a lawsuit) who has to bring in the evidence.

2. The right of the patient is to receive care according to average, reasonable and prudent standards. This means that the patient is not entitled to the *best* standards, but only to those of the average, reasonable and prudent person in the same profession as that of the defendant (the person or facility being sued). In other words, the defendant is required only to live up to the standards that would ordinarily be followed by his or her profession or type of institution. If the defendant is an obstetrician, for example, the standards required would be those of the average, reasonable and prudent obstetrician.

3. The standards to which the patient is entitled vary depending on the circumstances. If, for example, the patient was in an emergency situation, various tests or precautions that would ordinarily be average practice may not have been followed because the delay would have further harmed the patient. That the standard of care followed in such circumstances was lower does not mean that there was negligence. In the specific circumstances, the required standard may have been met, even though in other circumstances the standards would have been higher.

4. The fact that the defendant has made a mistake does not in itself mean that there has been negligence. Since most health care providers are in the business of making judgements, it must be expected that some of those judgements will be wrong. As long as the judgement was made in the proper way — that is, the appropriate information

was collected and considered — the required standards have been met, even though the patient may have been injured.

Not every doctor will make the same judgement in the same set of circumstances. That another doctor would have arrived at a different conclusion does not mean that one is negligent. In hindsight, it is easy to say that if a different decision had been made, the patient would not have been injured. Obviously, the decision made was wrong. Yet if it was made according to average, reasonable and prudent standards, the person making it has lived up to required legal standards and is not negligent.

Even if a doctor or other health professional makes a decision or does something that most in the same profession would not do, that action is not negligence. There may be a number of average, reasonable and prudent ways of doing something. That a profession is divided in its opinion on how something is to be done or what decision is to be made does not make one opinion the right one and all others negligent.

5. Even when all appropriate standards have been met, accidents still take place. This does not mean that the accident was due to negligence. The patient is entitled to have care and treatment that will attempt to avoid causing all reasonably foreseeable injury. If such care was given, there is no negligence, even though an accident occurred and the patient was injured.

6. A further complication arises because as time goes by standards change. The patient is entitled to receive care according to the standards that were average, reasonable and prudent at the time that care or treatment was received, not at the time the patient sues. When a trial takes place, the court must determine what the standards were, not what they are at present. The result of this principle is that every caregiver has a legal obligation to the patient to abide by currently accepted standards. It is not enough to have graduated with excellent credentials. There is a legal obligation throughout one's professional life to meet the constantly changing standards. Continuing education, therefore, is necessary. Similarly, even the most modern institutions have an obligation to modify equipment and techniques to meet current standards. A small hospital forty years ago may have

had a thriving obstetrical service. At present, that hospital may not be able to meet the new standards. Failing to meet those modern standards and causing injury is negligence, whereas forty years ago the same services would not have been considered negligent. The hospital is therefore under an obligation to the patient to either modify its service to meet modern standards or, if it cannot, to stop offering that service.

7. The most difficult consequence of the definition of negligence is that there must be injury or death and that the injury or death must be reasonably foreseeable. Therefore, if there has been a failure to meet average, reasonable and prudent standards but there has been no injury or death, or the injury or death was not reasonably foreseeable, or the injury or death could not be shown to be the possible consequence of the failure to meet the standards, there has been no negligence, though there may have been bad practice for which the patient cannot successfully sue.

The result is that a patient may receive poor and even seriously substandard care, but if the injury part of the equation has not been fulfilled, there is no negligence according to the law, and the plaintiff is not entitled to receive any compensation. This means that a patient is not entitled to compensation for poor care, insensitive care or even unprofessional care without the additional elements of the negligence equation.

The courts are fairly flexible in linking the injury to the substandard care. They do not have to have scientific proof that the injury resulted from the lack of care. If on the balance of probabilities the injury is most likely to have been a result, this may be accepted by the court.

Similarly, a patient may be injured or even die, but unless the injury or death is a result of the failure to meet the required standards, there is no negligence, and therefore no right to compensation. Once again, all parts of the equation must be fulfilled.

The Burden on the Plaintiff
Because of how negligence is defined, and because the plaintiff has to prove negligence, a lawsuit in which a person sues for negligence is

difficult, time consuming, expensive and often emotionally traumatic. It is for this reason that so few unhappy patients commence legal actions. (See chapter 22, "Why Don't Patients Sue?")

Unlike in a criminal case, in which the Crown must prove to the court "beyond a reasonable doubt" that the accused committed the crime, a civil action is not quite so onerous. The plaintiff still has the burden of proof, but only to convince the court that the defendant failed in the legal duty to the plaintiff, for which the plaintiff should be compensated. The court listens to the evidence presented by the plaintiff and weighs it against the evidence presented by the defendant. The "weightier" side wins. This means that a plaintiff may win a suit even though the court has a reasonable doubt about the merits of the claim, whereas in a criminal case any doubt must result in a finding of not guilty even if the Crown's position carries more weight than that of the accused.

The plaintiff has to prove each element of the negligence claim as follows:

1. *The facts.* The plaintiff brings evidence before the court of what he or she says happened. This is done by the plaintiff taking the witness stand and relating the facts as he remembers them in response to questions asked by his own lawyer and cross-examination by the opposing counsel. The judge may also ask questions to clarify any matters that are not clear. In addition, the plaintiff and the defendant may bring in witnesses who have personal knowledge of the facts.

Both sides are entitled to bring in documents that outline what may have happened. In fact, these documents, particularly medical or patient records, may be more valuable than the testimony given by witnesses. The records, although not necessarily correct, at least do not change over time. Witnesses, on the other hand, tend to forget or become confused, especially given that the trial invariably takes place two or more years after the event occurred. The witnesses may have been emotionally involved in the event or the aftermath, or after being questioned on so many occasions by lawyers in preparation for trial, they no longer are clear about what really happened. Even if the witnesses are telling the truth, the judge or the jury may not believe them. Patient records do not present this problem. If there is a conflict between the opposing sides as to what happened, the court must determine who to believe and try to reconstruct the facts.

2. *The standards.* The plaintiff must then advise the court as to what the average, reasonable and prudent standards were in the circumstances. These standards may be standards of how a particular diagnosis is arrived at, or how a particular nursing, physiotherapy or surgical procedure is performed. They may relate to what an average, reasonable and prudent nurse should have observed in particular circumstances, and to what such a nurse should have done as a result.

These standards have to be proven by the plaintiff. This is done usually by hiring an expert who appears as a witness and gives an opinion of what the appropriate standards were at the time. To be an expert, such a person has to be qualified to give an opinion in that discipline and to have the expertise of what is going on in that discipline. A doctor, for example, would not be qualified to give an expert opinion on the standards of a particular nursing technique. A paediatrician could not appear as an expert in a case involving gynaecology.

It is also not enough for such a person to be an expert in the field and be able to say what he or she would have done in the circumstances. The expert is to advise the court what the average, reasonable and prudent person in the field would have done, even though in some instances the expert may disagree with the standard practice.

This does not mean that the common practice of people in a particular field necessarily meets the standard that the court will apply to the case before it. As a general rule, however, this is what happens. On rare occasions the court may say that it does not think that the common practice is reasonable and therefore will not apply it. That, however, is unusual, since judges are not qualified to judge whether the practice of a particular profession is or is not reasonable.

The standards may also be derived from publications or policies of professional groups or institutions. They may also be derived from articles in professional journals and texts on the subject.

Often the experts disagree, and the court must decide between them. Frequently, the opinion of an expert will be discounted because it is given in hindsight. What the court really wants to know is what the average, reasonable and prudent person in that discipline or specialty would have done *at the time*. It is not enough to say that the defendant should have done something else now that the outcome and facts are fully known.

Expert testimony may also not be accepted because the expert did not have the advantage of having the full set of facts. In other situations the expert opinion may be reflective of one approach within a profession. Other approaches may well be accepted by many within the discipline. This means that no single approach may be considered negligent. Any one of them would have been average, reasonable, and prudent at the time, even though, as it turned out, one may have been wrong and even may have caused injury to the patient.

3. *Failure to meet the standards.* The experts are also brought in to give testimony and advise the court as to whether, based on the facts, the defendant failed to meet the standards required. It is therefore not enough to prove what the standards were; it must also be proved that they were not met.

Many of the problems of experts' testimony as noted previously apply equally to testimony on this point. Once the court has been informed of what the standards are to be applied to the facts, the experts must give their opinion as to whether there was a failure on the part of the defendant to meet those standards given the circumstances.

4. *Injury as a result.* The plaintiff then must bring evidence before the court that he or she was injured and that the injury was a reasonably foreseeable result of the failure of the defendant to meet the appropriate standards. This is a two-part process. First, the plaintiff brings witnesses or medical reports or both, along with his or her own testimony, to show that an injury has occurred. In the case of a death, the person suing on account of the death brings evidence that the person has in fact died.

The second aspect of the process is to bring to the court medical experts who are prepared to testify that the act of the defendant was the cause, or the most likely cause, of the injury or death. This is a particularly difficult exercise, since in many instances it is difficult to separate the original injury or illness of the plaintiff or the deceased from the treatment or care that may have caused the injury complained of, or at least added to it.

Experts in this area are frequently of a different specialty than the experts who testify about the standards of care required. For example, if a dentist is sued for negligence, a dental expert would be required to advise the court of the appropriate dental standards and whether the defendant had met them. Yet it may be necessary to have a neurologist testify whether the plaintiff suffered nerve damage and whether that damage could have been caused by what the dentist did.

5. *Compensation.* Finally, the plaintiff must provide evidence to support the claim for compensation that is the object of the negligence suit. A plaintiff seeks two types of compensation. The first is referred to as special damages and comprises those money items that can be specifically identified and have an exact dollar figure placed on them. It includes medical care that was paid for by the patient and any other actual costs or economic losses that can be measured exactly.

In addition, the plaintiff claims for general damages, which includes a projected loss of income, plus items such as loss of enjoyment and amenities of life, as well as pain and suffering. These items are determined by actuarial projections if loss of future income or future costs such as institutional care that might be required for the remainder of a person's life are involved. The general damages that cannot be expressed in precise money terms are determined by the court after examining the amounts given in previous cases involving similar injuries. These are the amounts that receive wide publicity in the United States when awards amounting to millions of dollars are given. In Canada, although the amount of the awards has been increasing, a certain damper has been placed on them by the Supreme Court of Canada. (See chapter 22, "Why Don't Patients Sue?")

The Law of the Good Samaritan
Ordinarily, apart from those who are involved in automobile accidents, there is no legal requirement to be a good Samaritan, that is, to voluntarily come to the assistance of another person. For this rea-

son a doctor, nurse or any other health professional is quite at liberty to pass by the scene of an accident or injury and do nothing, even though this may be considered unethical. This is a perfect example of how the law reflects the reality of how society acts, and not how one would like society to act.

However, once a person becomes a good Samaritan, the law does step in and requires that the helper act in an average, reasonable and prudent manner. If the good Samaritan has a special expertise, such as being a doctor, nurse or paramedic, the standards must be those of that discipline in the same or similar circumstances.

Many doctors have been concerned about the possibility of being sued in such circumstances. They recognize that in an emergency situation on the side of a highway, for instance, they cannot achieve the standards of care that would be expected of them in the emergency department of a hospital with equipment, drugs and support staff. What they fail to realize is that the law does not expect them to achieve those standards and the patient has no right to those standards. What the law does require is that they meet average, reasonable and prudent standards of care *in the circumstances*. The circumstances determine what is reasonable. There are no reports of cases in which anyone has sued a doctor or other health professional in a good Samaritan situation.

None the less, many health professionals are reluctant to be good Samaritans. This fear was largely one that arose in the United States, where health professionals are far more aware of the threat of malpractice suits than in Canada. The continental European approach to this problem is that by law, health professionals — and in fact every individual — is required to abide by the accepted ethical standard and to assist others in need at the scene of an emergency or obtain assistance. The American approach was to protect those who became good Samaritans from malpractice suits in the hope that they would no longer have an excuse to avoid these situations and would act accordingly. It is doubtful whether in fact this has worked.

As so often happens in Canada, Canadians, including Canadian physicians, react not to the realities in this country but to the highly publicized problems of the United States. They then search for American solutions to apply to problems that do not exist here. As a result, a number of Canadian provinces have adopted so-called good Samaritan acts.

The legislation in each province is somewhat different. In some cases protection applies only to doctors, in other cases it applies to all good Samaritans. In any event, it is usually restricted to acts of gross negligence. This means that if a doctor stops at the scene of an accident and is negligent, he cannot be held legally responsible for any injury he causes, unless he is very greatly negligent. No one is too clear about what those words mean, but they seem to imply that the doctor's conduct would have to either amount to wanton and reckless misconduct, or be totally without any concern for the patient.

From a patient's point of view, this is a serious removal of a patient's rights. It means that a doctor or a nurse who stops at the scene of an accident and renders care does not have to live up to the ordinary standards of medical or nursing care expected in such circumstances. Any injury caused by this good Samaritan would go uncompensated unless the conduct is gross.

Given the lobbying on behalf of civil rights organizations, one must wonder how such legislation was ever passed, and why Canada does not adopt the European approach.

The Thing Speaks for Itself

Although the patient-turned-plaintiff has an enormous burden to prove his or her case, there is a rule that in certain instances eases the burden. In Latin it is referred to as *res ipsa loquitur;* that is, *the thing speaks for itself.*

The rule is applied in those situations in which the plaintiff does not know what happened and has no way of finding out. Therefore, he cannot prove that what happened failed to meet the appropriate standards. Such a situation ordinarily would arise in surgery or in intensive care when the patient was unconscious. All the patient knows is that he entered into the situation in which the defendant was in control and he came out injured.

The rule applies in situations such as that of the "retained sponge," in which a sponge is left inside the patient after surgery, or if the patient fell off the operating table. Ordinarily these do not occur unless someone has been negligent.

To invoke the rule, the plaintiff must prove to the satisfaction of the judge that the defendant was in complete control of the situation *and* that ordinarily injury does not occur unless there has been negligence. If the judge is convinced that these two criteria have been met, the rule will apply, and the fact that the injury occurred is evidence that there was negligence. It does not mean that there was definitely negligence, but only that there is evidence of negligence. If the defendant does not produce any evidence to the contrary, the court is entitled to find that there was negligence.

In this sometimes rather confusing swing of evidence back and forth, some think that the onus is on the defendant to prove that he was not guilty. This is in fact not the case. All the defendant has to do is to provide evidence, usually by experts in the field, that shows that the injury could have occurred either by negligence or by some other means. This means that on one hand there is the plaintiff's case, which assumes negligence, and on the defendant's side there is evidence to show that it could have been negligence or not. If the court accepts the defendant's position, the onus goes back to the plaintiff to prove negligence, coming to the conclusion that "the thing" did not speak for itself.

Big Town versus Small Town

It is sometimes thought that the standards to which a patient is entitled are higher in a city hospital than in a small-town hospital. In fact, judges often will say that they are comparing the conduct of a family physician who is being sued with the standards of the average family physician in a town of similar size, or the standards of a small-town hospital with other hospitals in small towns.

The judges have become totally confused on this issue and have been affected by an old American legal rule called the locality rule, in which the standards applied to a defendant doctor in a particular town could only be taken from what the average practice was in that town. Eventually, the rule was discarded on the basis that doctors and others receive educational material and attend conferences in which standards are set across the country.

Therefore, that a hospital is in a small town does not by itself mean that its standards are lower than those of a city hospital. In fact, the standards of care in a small-town emergency department for an uncomplicated laceration may be better than the standards for the same injury on a Saturday night in the emergency department of a downtown urban hospital, where such an injury would have to wait behind the shootings, heart attacks, rapes and car accidents, before eventually being treated by an overworked intern. In other situations, a large city may provide higher standards because of the availability of specialized services.

The standard depends, therefore, not on whether the services are in a small town or a large city but on what the circumstances were at the time. The issue is what was average, reasonable and prudent in the circumstances.

Family Doctor versus Specialist

Many medical services are performed by both family physicians, or what have traditionally been called general practitioners, and specialists. The issue arises whether a patient has a right to a higher standard from a specialist. This is not necessarily so. If the procedure in question is carried out at the same standard by both the family doctor and the specialist, the patient has no right to insist on higher standards from the specialist. The defence is that if there is one way to perform a procedure regardless of who does it, standards are uniform.

If, however, only the specialist could be expected to know what to do, the patient cannot complain that the family physician did not meet those standards. Yet the complaint may be that the family physician was negligent in failing to consult a specialist, or negligent in taking on the procedure that only a specialist should perform.

A number of years ago, family doctors performed many procedures that now only specialists perform. Therefore, the standard of care that the patient is now entitled to, that of a specialist, is higher than that to which the patient was earlier entitled under a family doctor.

Examples of Negligence

Negligence can come about either by an omission or a commission. The defendant health professional may be negligent by not doing something that ought to have been done, by doing something that ought not to have been done or by doing something in an improper manner.

Negligence may have occurred in a number of ways, including:

1. providing negligent care or treatment in the course of a procedure

2. negligently deciding to perform a particular course of treatment

3. failing to carry out a particular procedure or treatment

4. failing to consult a specialist

5. failing to bring in assistance

6. giving a negligent diagnosis

7. failing to properly advise the patient regarding care

8. improperly discharging the patient

Negligence can occur in many ways. It can, for example, be the failure to conduct the diagnostic procedure in an appropriate manner resulting in injury because of a delayed diagnosis. In 1990, the case of *Heenan v. Winner* was heard by the Supreme Court of British Columbia. Madeline Hennan broke her leg and hip while skiing. At the hospital, Dr. J.M. Winner, a general practitioner at the Matsqui-Sumas-Abbotsford General Hospital ordered x-rays, but despite the order, x-rays of the hip were not taken. The patient and her husband both mentioned that she thought she had injured the hip. Twenty-seven hours later, she was x-rayed at Delta Hospital, and was then transferred to Richmond Hospital where her fracture was treated. Four corrective operations were necessary.

The court found Dr. Winner's negligence "inescapable and almost inexplicable." The court found that he had failed to meet the required standard of care of a family physician in that institution because of his inept physical examination and his failure to realize that he had received an incomplete set of x-rays. In addition, the technician at the hospital was negligent in not providing the x-rays required in the hospital's own procedure manual. However, Dr. Winner could have overcome this negligence by asking for the proper x-rays. The court concluded that Dr. Winner's negligence caused the delay in diagnosis resulting in the subsequent problems and necessary operations. The hospital was also held responsible for the pain and suffering inflicted by its staff.

Summary of Principles

1. Every patient receiving health services has a right to receive those services according to average, reasonable and prudent standards.

2. A patient does not have the right to receive services according to the best standards available.

3. A patient who does not receive services according to average, reasonable and prudent standards and as a result suffers reasonably foreseeable injury has a right to be compensated for that injury on the basis of negligence. (A surviving family member may be compensated for the death of the patient.)

4. The patient does not have the right to be compensated for services that have not met proper standards when there has been no injury as a result.

5. The patient does not have the right to be compensated for an injury (or the survivors for a death) resulting from the services if the appropriate standards have been met.

6. A patient has no right to be compensated for an injury from health services if that injury arose from an error in judgement.

7. In any claim for compensation for negligent care, the onus is on the patient to prove to the satisfaction of the court on the balance of probabilities that there has been negligence, and not on the defendant to prove that there has not been negligence.

6

WHO IS

RESPONSIBLE

FOR

WHOM?

Individual Responsibility

EVERYONE WHO GIVES CARE OR TREATMENT to a patient, either directly or indirectly, has a personal responsibility to that patient. This includes not only those people the patient has a personal relationship with, such as the doctor, nurse, therapist or orderly, but many people in the health system the patient never sees. Laboratory technologists, dietitians, health record administrators, and clerks provide patient services but may never encounter the patient.

Any one of these individuals, whether they are self-employed or employees of an institution, clinic, medical group or another individual, is personally and directly responsible to the patient for the consequences of any wrongful act affecting the patient. It may be negligence, or it may be an intentional wrong such as assault, defamation or false imprisonment.

Traditionally, however, the law felt that when someone enters into a contract with another for services, and the person providing the services does so by employing someone else to do it, the recipient of the services should not have to search to find who did the work and caused the injury. When a patient enters hospital for various services, the contract is between the patient and the hospital. The hospital employs hundreds or even thousands to carry out those services. This is not the patient's problem. The patient can look to the hospital to make certain that all duties are fulfilled. The hospital as an employer cannot pass the buck. However, the individual employee still is personally responsible and can also be sued directly by the patient and be held responsible individually.

Another practical problem in suing employees is financial. Usually, employees could not afford to compensate a plaintiff for injury, whereas the employer was more likely to be able to do so. Over the years, however, it was recognized that in many instances an employee was not necessarily so financially strapped as not to be able to satisfy the judgement of a court. Many employees own homes, cars, cottages, stocks and bonds. As a result, many health care professionals carry their own private malpractice insurance, even though they are employees of institutions that also carry insurance. (See "What about Insurance?" in this chapter.)

Responsibility for Employees

The patient who sues a hospital, nursing home, home care agency or clinic does not have to look for the person who supposedly caused the injury. As far as the patient is concerned, the injury was caused by the organization or person who agreed to provide the service.

However, the plaintiff does have a choice and can sue the institution, or the employee who supposedly did the wrongful act, or both. A number of employees may be named as defendants. If, as the legal proceedings carry on, it turns out that some were not in fact involved, they can always be dropped as defendants. Rules of procedure make it much more difficult to add new defendants than to drop some.

These practices rest on the basic legal principle that was traditionally called the master-servant rule. This held that the "master" or employer is responsible for the wrongful acts performed by the "servant" or employee that were performed in the course of the employment. This meant that as long as the employee was carrying out the employer's obligations to provide services to the plaintiff, the employer was responsible for those acts.

A hospital admits a patient and provides nursing care, dietary services, laboratory services and maintenance, and is therefore responsible for any wrongful act such as negligence in the provision of those services. The same is true when a patient visits a doctor's office and is injured by the nurse employed by the doctor, or by a dental assistant employed by a dentist. A number of issues arise, however, that could affect the right of a patient to sue an employer.

The first of these concerns the employee who disobeys the employer's instructions, such as a physiotherapist employed by a clinic who has been told not to use a malfunctioning piece of equipment but who does so and injures the patient. That the physiotherapist disobeyed the employer's instructions does not release the employer from the responsibility for the employee. If the employee goes beyond the scope of the job, ordinarily the employer is still responsible, since as far as the patient is concerned the employee is.

The only exception to this rule is that the employer is not responsible for employees who are off on what the courts have called a "frolic" of their own. This would be a circumstance in which an employee is clearly not acting as an employee. For example, if a nurse after work hours, and not in uniform, took a nursing home or hospital patient out for a drive and acted in such a manner that the patient was injured, it would be difficult to show that this act was performed while in the service of the employer.

In recent years, hospitals and nursing homes have not been providing various services to their parents or residents by using employees. Instead, they have contracted out those services. Many institutions no longer have employees to provide meals; they contract with a catering service. Patients who are injured by food poisoning because of the negligence of the dietary service can still look to the institution for compensation, since it is one of the services the institution has agreed to provide to the patient. The way the institution has arranged to provide those services is not the patient's problem.

However, there are situations in which the institution makes it quite clear that certain services provided during a patient's stay are not being provided by the hospital or nursing home, and that therefore the hospital is not responsible for them. This may include certain diagnostic services such as x-rays, or a hairdressing service.

As home care becomes increasingly popular with governments restricting the availability of hospitals, many people hire nurses, nursing assistants or licensed practical nurses, or health aides or personal care workers through private agencies. In some instances, the patient or client is contracting with the agency for these services and the agency provides them. In such a situation, the agency is responsible for those services. However, the contract with the agency may be that the client is actually hiring the individual and the agency simply finds the individual and sets up the arrangement. In these circumstances, the agency may not be responsible. In this situation, the agency would be responsible only if it was negligent in placing a person with a client. This could come about if the agency placed with a client a person who was not trained to perform certain tasks that were requested by the client.

Responsibility for Doctors

At one time, hospitals were not responsible for the wrongful acts of their doctors or nurses even when these people were employees. The theory was that an employer could be responsible only for the actions of employees whom the employer could control. The employer had to have control over *what* the employee did and *how* the employee did it. In the case of doctors and very often nurses, the employer could tell these employees *what* to do but not *how* to do it, since these people were professionals who had to make judgements depending on the circumstances. How a certain procedure was to be carried out had to be left to the professional involved.

When an institution such as a hospital hires doctors and nurses, it is contracting with the patient to offer medical and nursing services. In providing these services, the hospital has a duty to the patient to provide these services according to average, reasonable and prudent standards. Failure to meet these standards is a breach of the hospital's obligation to the patient, as well as a breach of the employee's obligation.

The reality in Canada is that almost all nurses are employees of someone. They carry out the responsibilities taken on by hospitals, long-term-care institutions, group homes, public health organizations, home care agencies, clinics and educational facilities as well as corporations. These institutions are therefore responsible for the work performed by nurses as part of their employment.

Most doctors, however, are not employees, though this situation is changing. Hospitals are hiring more doctors in specialized services such as emergency departments. Psychiatric hospitals tend to hire a significant number of physicians to make up their medical staffs. Still, the majority of physicians who base all or part of their practice in a hospital are not employees but have been granted the privilege of using hospital facilities, supplies, equipment and staff to treat their patients. These physicians, in addition to those who hold medical staff privileges but are also employees of the hospital, make up the hospital medical staff. Many long-term-care institutions also have an organized medical staff. (See chapter 2, "The Right to a Doctor of One's Choice.")

Canadian law has for a very long time been clear in stating that a hospital is not responsible for the physicians on the medical staff who are not employees of the hospital. These physicians are not acting on behalf of the hospital but are retained privately by the patient. In case after case, the courts refused to hold hospitals legally responsible for the wrongdoing of independently employed physicians.

The American courts some years ago began moving away from this position and have held hospitals responsible for private doctors on their staffs. This has occurred in two circumstances. The first is the situation in which a hospital itself has been negligent in granting privileges to a doctor. It may have not properly screened the doctor to verify that he or she had the qualifications for the privileges being granted. The doctor is given privileges and injures a patient when exercising privileges that should not have been granted. The injury could have been foreseen. Negligence is found on the part of the hospital and perhaps on the part of the doctor. Both are held responsible. The doctor is held personally liable. The hospital is held responsible not vicariously — that is, as an employer would be held responsible — but because of its own negligence.

American hospitals have also been held liable for their negligence in not properly auditing their medical staff members. If a physician on the staff is not adhering to proper standards, American hospitals have a duty to know this through a regular audit system, which examines such matters as the length of time patients with various ailments have stayed in hospital and the return rate to the operating room for complications. These audits can be complicated because every patient reacts differently to different procedures and to different illnesses. However, medical audits can identify problems with a particular doctor for at least assessment and closer examination.

If a hospital does not audit its doctors, or if the audits are done improperly, it may be said that patient injuries caused by doctors could have been foreseen and avoided by altering or removing the privileges of those doctors. Failures to do so may be considered negligence on the part of the hospital.

Canadian courts have not had to deal with this problem except in a few isolated incidents.

Patients should seek compensation for medical malpractice from doctors, not from hospitals, alleging that the hospitals allowed it to take place. The reason is that hospitals usually require their medical staff to be insured or protected through the Canadian Medical Protective Association. Therefore, there is no need for a plaintiff to prove not only that the doctor was negligent but also that the hospital was negligent in allowing the doctor's negligence to take place. Such an effort would be extremely expensive and time consuming, since various experts would have to be brought in to testify that the hospital knew or ought to have known that the doctor might be negligent and cause patient injury. Yet with Canadian lawyers being increasingly influenced by the creativity of their American colleagues, and Canadian courts under greater and greater influence of American judicial thinking, the future course of the law may be very different than in the past. The American approach could be followed in Canada, or at least influence Canadian law.

Are Doctors Responsible for Nurses (and Others)?

At one time there was a legal theory called "the captain of the ship doctrine." Under this doctrine a surgeon in an operating room was "the captain of the ship" and was totally responsible for what everyone else did, in particular what the operating room nurses did. The theory was that whereas the hospital ordinarily might be responsible for the nurses it employed, it could be responsible for them only when it had control over what they did. It was felt that when the doors of the operating room closed, the hospital lost control, which was passed to the surgeon. If there was any nursing malpractice, the patient would seek compensation for the surgeon who had "borrowed" them rather than from the employer of the nurses. As a result, it was also called the borrowed servant rule. This is not the law in Canada.

When a hospital admits a patient for surgery, it agrees to provide the patient with a number of services, including the services of operating room nurses. The nurses are of course responsible for their own actions, along with those of their employer, who has supplied their services to the patient.

It is clear that doctors are not legally responsible for nurses and other health professionals and staff even though they give "medical orders" to them. The only exception is if the doctor was to employ other personnel, which in fact occurs in a private medical office or clinic.

However, there are situations in which a doctor can be held responsible for what a nurse or other health care provider does, but not in the same way that an employer is responsible for the acts of an employee. An employer is responsible not because of any personal wrongdoing but because an employee acting on behalf of the employer has committed a wrong against the patient.

A doctor can be legally responsible for the wrongdoing of a nurse or other personnel when that wrongdoing arises out of the wrongful act of the doctor. If, for example, a doctor gives a medical order to a nurse knowing that the nurse is not permitted under nursing regulations to perform such a procedure, the nurse may have committed negligence, but so has the doctor. If the doctor was the nurse's employer, the doctor could be held liable on two counts: the first as an employer of the wrongfully acting nurse, the second for personal negligence in asking the nurse to do the act that injured the patient.

If a doctor asks a nurse to perform an act that the nurse knows falls below average, reasonable and prudent nursing standards, must the nurse follow the doctor's order? The answer is no. To do so, the nurse would be committing a negligent act. In fact, the nurse has a legal duty to the patient to refuse. Similarly, the doctor might also be committing negligence if it can be shown that the average, reasonable and prudent doctor would not have given a nurse such an order. On the other hand, if a nurse fails to follow a doctor's order when the average, reasonable and prudent nurse would have followed it, the nurse is responsible for any injury caused by such a negligent act. The doctor is not responsible, since doctors are entitled to assume that when they make a medical decision, the hospital staff will carry it out.

The entire relationship between doctors and other health professionals is one that is constantly changing and is often highly emotional, as medicine and other disciplines frequently come into conflict. Originally, doctors made all the decisions, and everyone else was there solely to assist the doctor. Over the years, however, other disciplines such as nursing developed expanded roles and increased education. They felt that they were equal members of the team and could act as independent professionals.

It is not always clear what this entails, except that patients are frequently caught in the middle of interdisciplinary disputes. The patient's right is to receive average, reasonable and prudent medical and nursing care. This may be fine in principle, but it is not always clear exactly what this care entails. There are many instances in which a nurse or other health professional can take action independently from that of the doctor, and in fact have a duty to the patient to do so.

Unfortunately, there is little that a patient can do when facing a situation in which a doctor and the hospital staff are not working as a team. The patient may become aware of the problem only on receiving one report from a doctor and a very different story from nurses, technologists or other doctors. (See chapter 21, "To Whom Do You Complain and How?")

Conflicts may also arise between pharmacists and doctors. A doctor may prescribe medication that is contraindicated (that is, it will conflict with another medication the patient is taking) or to which the patient is allergic. That the doctor prescribed the medication does not obligate the pharmacist to dispense it. In fact, if the pharmacist knows of the situation, there is a duty to the patient to not dispense the medication and to contact the doctor.

Part of the difficulty in this case is that many people use more than one pharmacy. Therefore, no pharmacist may have the complete picture and cannot be obligated to the patient in this way. If all medications are dispensed through one pharmacy, however, the patient can expect this level of professional service.

If a doctor writes a medical order or a prescription that the nurse, pharmacist, or other health care provider cannot understand, or cannot read, they would also have a legal obligation to the patient to contact the physician to clarify the order. Failure to do so, which may result in patient injury, could be considered negligence. It may be said that a doctor is surely negligent for issuing illegible instructions. However, the doctor is probably entitled to assume that if the writing is not understood, the reader will ask for clarification. It would be difficult to hold a doctor responsible for somebody carrying out the doctor's order according to what they thought the order said, when with a simple question the matter could have been clarified.

If a professional dispute breaks out between health professionals, there is a structure in the hospital for resolution. Depending on the hospital, this structure may be quite informal or quite sophisticated. From the medical side, the matter should be referred to the head of the department, chief of staff or medical director. On the nursing side, the director of nursing should become involved. During these disputes, the professionals often focus on protecting their own rights and interests, and the rights of the patients are left behind. The patient does not have a right to tell them how to practise medicine, nursing, physiotherapy, pharmacy or whatever it may be, nor to tell a hospital how to administer its affairs. However, the patient does have a legal right to reasonable care and to care that avoids reasonably foreseeable injury. If such conflicts could possibly result in patient injury, the patient does have a right to have the situation corrected.

The difficulty is that the patient either does not know what is occurring or cannot do anything about it. This is where the legal system breaks down. The law invariably steps in only after injury occurs, when it is too late. The theory is that all the parties will know their legal rights and duties and therefore abide by them, thus avoiding such problems. In fact, the level of legal education among health professionals is shockingly low, and efforts are only now beginning to be made to prevent these situations from occurring, rather than to try to solve the insoluble after a patient is injured.

Split Responsibility

In many cases responsibility is divided among a number of people. It cannot be said that one doctor, one nurse or any other one individual was the sole cause of the patient's injury. It is possible for a court to divide the responsibility among various defendants in various proportions. There is no scientific way of determining whether one defendant is 30 percent at fault or 50 percent or 10 percent. It simply depends on how the judge or the jury views it.

In addition, it may be found that the patient was also partially to blame for the injuries, in which case the total amount of compensation awarded will be decreased by that percentage.

It is possible, therefore, to have a rather complicated scenario. A pedestrian without watching for traffic steps into a busy street and is struck by a car. The driver of the car was talking to a passenger in the back seat and did not see the pedestrian. The pedestrian was taken to the hospital where he was x-rayed and released on the basis that there was nothing wrong. The x-rays were in fact never read because the x-ray technologist mixed them up with other x-rays. The patient subsequently became partially paralysed because of the failure of the hospital to make certain that the x-rays were read and of the attending physician to check whether they in fact were read. The doctor should have known that they were not read.

It is possible in such a situation for the patient (now plaintiff) to be found 25 percent at fault, the driver of the car 30 percent, the technologist 15 percent and the doctor 30 percent. The hospital is responsible for the technologist's share along with the technologist personally. Translating this into money if the damages awarded were $100,000, the driver owes the patient $30,000, the hospital owes him $15,000 and the doctor owes him $30,000. The patient therefore gets only 75 percent of the value of his injuries.

Whom Do You Sue?

When a disgruntled patient visits a lawyer, seeking advice on what the patient thinks is questionable conduct, the patient either is determined to sue a particular person or has no idea who might be legally responsible. It is the lawyer who analyses the situation and determines the relationship between the patient and anyone or any corporation who might have had a legal duty to the patient, and whether that duty might have been breached. In the end, it is the lawyer who determines who is going to be sued, barring any instructions to the contrary from the client, the patient-turned-plaintiff. If anyone who might conceivably be at least partially at fault is left out and the court determines that they are at fault to a certain degree, the plaintiff will lose that percentage of the award, since the award can be enforced only against those who have been named defendants.

In order to be on the safe side, there is a tendency on the part of lawyers to sue everyone in sight. These defendants can easily be dropped from the suit later if the case against them is obviously not going to succeed. It is this shotgun technique that results in a long list of defendants, usually including the employer and every conceivable employee who may have been involved in the matter.

The only problem with such an approach is that every defendant must have legal counsel, usually appointed by the various insurance companies for the defendants. This of course raises costs enormously for the entire health care system. If the bringing of suits is obviously frivolous, the court may penalize the plaintiff by requiring the plaintiff to pay the defendants' costs. However, "costs" according to the law rarely covers the actual costs of a defence.

What about Insurance?

To protect themselves, and in doing so protect patients, health care institutions and many health professionals carry malpractice insurance. Institutions such as hospitals have traditionally purchased insurance on the open insurance market. Because of the rising costs, however, various other arrangements are being developed, with groups of institutions starting their own insurance funds sometimes with the assistance of provincial governments, and sometimes with partial insurance coverage.

Most physicians in Canada do not carry private malpractice insurance, though it is available. Most belong instead to the Canadian Medical Protective Association, or CMPA. The CMPA is not an insurance company, though it carries out the same role in the sense that it defends doctors who are sued for malpractice and settles or pays those claims it believes are legally supportable. It is patterned after similar organizations in the United Kingdom, such as the Medical Defence Union, which at one time did take in Canadian members but no longer operates in Canada or in the United States.

The theory has been that a private insurance company is motivated by profit and that it therefore will frequently make its decisions on the basis of financial considerations and not on whether the doctor would be found legally responsible by a court. In small cases, the thought is that a private insurer may pay a patient claimant purely on its nuisance value. It is cheaper to settle the claim than to fight, because of the high legal costs of a dispute that could drag on for years. In larger claims it may be cheaper to fight, in the hope that the plaintiff as an individual (and one who has been injured) will simply run out of money. Legal stalling may force the plaintiff to give up the fight or to settle for less than would be awarded by a court if the matter went to trial.

Because the CMPA is non-profit and exists solely to assist its members, it should be basing decisions on whether it thinks the doctor was in fact at fault and legally responsible. It will defend a doctor it feels is blameless regardless of the costs and will settle if it feels there is legal responsibility.

However, the CMPA has been feeling the pinch of vastly increasing costs. The problem is not that the number of claims against doctors has risen so dramatically in Canada over the past few years. It is that the legal costs of obtaining advice and negotiating have skyrocketed, along with the size of the awards given by the courts and therefore the amounts for which claims must be settled.

Among many plaintiffs' lawyers across Canada who are used to dealing with private insurance companies, many have found CMPA lawyers extremely conservative and overly defensive, causing enormous costs and delays by quite legal, procedural and other delaying tactics. In this sense the organization is doing its defensive duty to its members, though one must raise the question of whether this enhances the reputation of the profession.

Registered nurses have become aware that they are increasingly at risk of a malpractice suit. Even though they are almost all employees and are therefore protected by their employers, who carry malpractice insurance, there is always the possibility that a nurse may become personally liable. Since the nurse who is found to have breached a legal duty to a patient has also breached the duty to the employer, it is possible for the employer to take action to recover its costs against the nurse. The employer is unlikely to do this because of the labour disruption it would cause, but the employer's private insurer might not have any hesitation. Although this in fact has not been the practice, Canadian nurses were concerned enough to take matters into their own hands rather than rely on their employers' insurance companies.

The result was the establishment of the Canadian Nurses Protective Society, to which a high percentage of Canadian nurses belong. This organization offers to nurses secondary protection. If a nurse is sued, the nurse will look to the employer's insurer for protection. If for some reason that protection is not forthcoming, or if the insurer takes action against the nurse for compensation for the funds it had to pay out to pay out to a patient, then the society will step in.

Various other health disciplines in Canada carry group insurance even when their members may largely be employees.

The problem of insurance costs is constantly on the minds of health administrators in Canada. Among arrangements being developed to lower costs are elaborate programs of risk management designed to avoid, or at least reduce, the possibility of patient injury and thus the risk of exposure to patient claims and lawsuits. More than any legislation or lawsuits, this preventive program will prove to be the most effective in protecting patients' rights.

In addition, a recommendation was made in the 1990 task force report *Liability and Compensation in Health Care* to the conference of deputy ministers of health of the federal, provincial and territorial governments. It recommended that a no-fault compensation scheme be established for persons suffering significant avoidable health care injuries that would be available to injured patients as an alternative to pursuing a negligence action for medical malpractice. So far, the governments have done nothing.

Summary of Principles

1. Every person who provides health services to a patient has a personal duty to that patient regardless of whether the provider is self-employed or employed by someone else.

2. The patient may seek compensation for injuries caused by negligent health services from either the employee who caused the injuries, or from the employer, or from both.

3. A hospital is not ordinarily responsible for the wrongful acts of a member of its medical staff unless that physician is also an employee of the hospital.

4. Doctors are not legally responsible for the wrongful acts of nurses or other personnel, including other doctors, unless the doctor who issued the orders or was supervising the other personnel was also negligent.

5. Responsibility to a patient may be shared among a number of parties.

TREATMENT

OF

CHILDREN

A S WITH SO MANY OTHER aspects of health law, there is a long-standing myth that children are legally incapable of consenting to their own medical treatment. As a general rule, this is not true. Yet to say that all children can consent to all treatment under all conditions is also untrue.

Children are people. They have the same legal rights as adults. They do not, however, always have the same duties or responsibilities.

As with any other person receiving medical or surgical or any other health care or treatment, children have the basic right to receive services at an average, reasonable and prudent standard and to be protected from reasonably foreseeable injuries. (See chapter 5, "Negligence and Standards of Care.") As with an adult patient, the standards of care owed to a child patient vary with the circumstances. Because the patient is a child, there will be certain standards relating to paediatric care that do not apply to the care of adults.

It is often assumed that children cannot consent to their own medical or surgical treatment until they have reached the age of majority. (This varies among the provinces but is usually 18 or 19.) This is not true, although many hospitals believe it true and insist upon getting the consent of a patient's parents.

The courts have refused to set an age. Each case has been judged on its own merits, which means that a child can consent to treatment if that child has the mental capability of fulfilling the consent process for the treatment being proposed. This means that if a particular child understands that he or she has the right to refuse care or treatment, and understands the information given upon which the consent decision is made, that child has the legal right to consent to or refuse that particular procedure.

A child in that situation, therefore, is to be treated as an adult for consent purposes. The parents cannot give or refuse consent on the child's behalf. They do not have to be consulted and cannot overrule any decision made by the child. However, the hospital or doctor may as a condition of treatment require that the parents at least be told of and agree with the child's decision.

In a 1986 Alberta Court of Appeal case, *C. v. Wren,* the court ruled that a 16-year-old girl had sufficient intelligence and understanding to make up her own mind to consent to an abortion. Her parents' objections could not overrule her decision. This ruling does not mean that every 16-year-old can consent to an abortion, or to anything else. It simply means that this *particular* 16-year-old was able to consent to this *particular* procedure. It also does not mean that this 16-year-old necessarily had the mental capability to consent to other procedures.

Occasionally, reference is made to the so-called mature minor rule, whereby patients under the age of majority are regarded as adults and have their consent accepted by hospitals. An institution may take the consent of a minor who is living away from home but will not accept the consent of one who is still at home. This is not the law. Whether a person has a job or lives at home has nothing to do with the person's ability to consent to treatment. The determining factor is the mental capability of the person.

A number of provinces have attempted to pass legislation governing the age of consent rather than leave the law flexible. These various enactments set a particular age but then include exceptions depending on the circumstances.

For example, the Public Health Protection Act in Quebec sets the age of consent at 14 in a hospital and various other institutions. However, if the child is kept for more than twelve hours, the parents must be informed. New Brunswick, on the other hand, sets the age of 16, but does allow younger patients to consent if another physician or dentist gives a written opinion that the child is capable of understanding the nature and consequences of a medical treatment and that it is to be in the best interests of the child. The Ontario Consent to Treatment Act does concern itself with various ages but specifically preserves the right of a patient of any age to give or refuse consent to treatment if the patient is mentally capable of giving or refusing consent to that treatment. Other provinces have legislated on this issue, which has resulted in a great deal of confusion, and differences across the country. A child who is travelling, of course, is bound by the laws of the province or territory in which the treatment is being performed and not of the place where the child resides.

There is also a great deal of inconsistency within provinces. Nova Scotia does not have an age of consent in its legislation. The age depends on the mental maturity of the particular child. However, the Medical Consent Act of that province allows only people who are 19 or older to appoint someone to consent on their behalf if in the future they are not able to do so. This means that a 15- or 16-year-old child can consent to a particular medical or dental procedure if the child is mentally capable of doing so but is not permitted to appoint a substitute if that child should become mentally incapable of consenting.

A further situation illustrates society's confusion as to how it treats children. Where a child is in need of protection because of parental neglect or other causes, a government agency or the Children's Aid Society may take the child away from the parents and act as the parent. This may include consenting to medical treatment.

Child welfare legislation of this type sets the age below which this can take place. The problem is that if the age is, for example, 14, a child under this age may be mentally capable of consenting to certain treatment. The child welfare agency may step in and consent to treatment, but its consent is invalid because, for the purposes of consent, the child is to be treated as an adult and can consent or not without any parental intervention. The agency has only the authority that the parents would have had, and for consent purposes they do not have any. The conclusion, therefore, is that for one purpose the child is indeed a child in need of protection but for another purpose the child is to be treated as an adult.

A further problem arises if the child clearly cannot consent independently and requires the consent of a parent, but the parents disagree. If the parents are separated or divorced, the parent who is in charge or has custody makes the decision. If, however, the parents are together and disagree, the health care provider can accept the decision of either. The onus then rests with the parent who disagrees to take legal action to overturn the decision or to invoke child welfare legislation to protect the child.

The courts have put a further restriction on those who consent to treatment for persons who cannot consent on their own behalf. In 1986 the Supreme Court of Canada, in the case of *Re Eve,* prohibited a non-therapeutic sterilization of a mentally incompetent person on the grounds that in that particular case it was felt by the court that the procedure was not for the benefit of the individual. The principle is clear whether the person to be treated is mentally incompetent due to retardation or mentally incapable of consenting for some other reason, such as immaturity. This means that there may be situations in which a parent may not be permitted to consent to certain procedures on the basis that they are neither therapeutic nor for the benefit of the child. The question remains to determine what is meant by benefit.

The result is that children have far more rights to choose whether or not they are to have treatment, including such procedures as abortion and those involving life-saving treatment. However, the interference of legislation, while setting basic guidelines, may cause far more problems because of the difficulties in interpretation or in applying the exceptions invariably built in to the legislation.

Summary of Principles

1. Children have the legal right to average, standards of health care as it pertains to the
2. A child has the right to consent to or refuse treat... adult if the child has the mental capability of understanding what i. means to consent to treatment and understanding the information given before consent.
3. Restrictions on a child's right to consent to treatment may be included in provincial legislation.
4. If a child is not able to consent to or refuse treatment, a parent or a properly appointed substitute may consent on the child's behalf.
5. A person who is consenting on a child's behalf may not have the right to consent to a procedure that is non-therapeutic and that may not be considered for the benefit of the child.

8

THE
PATIENT'S
PROPERTY

ONE OF THE MOST ANNOYING INCIDENTS that can happen to any patient is the loss or damage of property while the patient is undergoing treatment. The disappearance of a raincoat in the doctor's waiting room, the theft of one's entire outer clothing while having x-rays, and the loss or breakage of dentures while in a hospital or nursing home are so common that many staff in health care facilities regard them as insignificant.

Eyeglasses, dentures and hearing aids are lost so frequently that the handling of the matter is a bureaucratic procedure. The patient may or may not be compensated, depending largely on how sensitive the facility is to patient annoyance. The more fuss a patient makes, the more expensive it becomes for an institution or its insurer to deal with the matter. In many cases, the attitude is, "For heaven's sake, here's some money. Just go away." Payment is made without admitting liability, and on a nuisance basis. The reason that liability is not admitted is that in many cases there *is* no liability. The health care facility is not legally responsible for a patient's belongings. If, however, a patient gives property to the hospital for safe-keeping, the patient has the right to expect the hospital to maintain reasonable care over the property. If, despite reasonable care the property is lost or damaged, the hospital is not responsible.

From the facility's point of view, patient property is a real headache. It does indeed interfere with the job of looking after the patient. Looking after the patient means looking after the patient's body — preferably naked. But despite warnings, advice and pleas, orally and in writing, patients arrive, particularly at hospital, loaded with stylish nightgowns, antique brooches, diamond watches, designer whatever imaginable — all the way to securities, cash, knives and guns.

Many losses occur when a patient arrives unexpectedly through the hospital emergency department and is stripped of various personal items, which may or may not be given to whoever happened to arrive with the patient, if anyone did. The patient is then transferred elsewhere in the hospital and may be moved around to surgery, postoperative care, intensive care and recovery rooms. There may be moves for x-rays or other diagnostic tests, during which watches and other personal items are removed and may be misplaced or left behind. Given all this moving about, it is almost a miracle that any patient is discharged with all personal items intact.

Theft is also not unknown. How would a patient know? Patients often have no idea where they are or where they have been. The thief could be a visitor, another patient or a staff member.

Even in long term care facilities, where a resident has moved in along with numerous household goods, theft or loss is far more frequent than administrators would like. Many residents are uncertain about what they own. Even with the most careful accounting on the part of staff, other items arrive with visitors — and then disappear. Residents are confused about when they owned something or even *if* they owned something. Some residents may have no concept of personal property and wander about helping themselves. Even the best-run long term care facility faces this problem.

Often, patients or residents whose property disappears do not complain. They may not even know that they have lost anything, or they just do not want to make a fuss. The attitude of many is, "I better not rock the boat. I may need the bedpan in the middle of the night."

Many complaints go unanswered. In other cases, patients are either compensated or the property is replaced, regardless of legal responsibility. This may be paid directly out of an institution's budget by the insurer. Lawsuits in these matters are not as common as one would imagine. Even when liability could be proven, most people feel that it is not worth the effort, even to go to small claims court.

The strong recommendation is, therefore, to not take anything to a hospital that you cannot afford to lose. Take only those things that are absolutely necessary, such as dentures, glasses and the minimum of clothing.

In out-patient clinics and doctors' and dentists' offices, hang on to purses and briefcases for dear life, and watch your property the way you would in any public place.

Summary of Principles

1. The patient has a right to have personal property given to a health institution for safe-keeping to be kept under reasonable care.

2. The health institution, clinic or office does not guarantee the safe-keeping of the patient's property.

3. The patient has the right to be compensated for lost or damaged property brought about by the negligence of a health facility or its employees.

9

PATIENT
RECORDS,
ACCESS AND
CONFIDENTIALITY

THE CORNERSTONE OF ANY health care institution, from a mammoth university teaching hospital to an outpatient physiotherapy clinic to a home care agency, is the patient record. At one time these documents were referred to as medical records and the personnel who filed them and kept them in order were called medical record librarians. In French they are referred to as *archivistes medicales*.

This terminology reflected the way these documents were regarded and the status held by those who dealt with them. The documents were simply files of reports dealing with the care and treatment of each patient. They were important but were used to a greater or lesser extent depending on who looked at them. The standards of care by which they were compiled were inconsistent across the country and within institutions. The medical record librarians had minimal training and were often regarded as filing clerks.

Within the past twenty years, however, it has been realized that with so many people becoming involved in the care and treatment of patients, it is essential to have an efficient and sophisticated means of communicating information among them.

It became vital to have doctors make their findings and opinions known to nurses and other personnel who would be carrying out treatment and care. Similarly, physicians would be basing their decisions on information conveyed to them by technologists, other health professionals, therapists of various types and by numerous automated pieces of equipment. To properly assess and monitor a patient's condition, therefore, information is required from a multitude of disciplines and diagnostic testing devices.

Because medical and other decisions will often be based on this information, it is essential that there is a highly sophisticated system of compiling the information, bringing it together and analysing it.

In addition, hospitals and government health insurance plans want to be able to analyse how health care is provided to ensure that it meets certain standards and that moneys are spent within the guidelines set by the government. In order to carry out what is called utilization management, a great deal of information must be collected on the number of procedures performed, the time required for each, the success rate and so on. This information is now also being used to determine whether physicians are practising in the hospital according to certain standards, and whether they should be granted a renewal of their hospital privileges.

To be able to do this, a new and highly trained discipline has emerged, that of the health record administrator. The Canadian College of Health Record Administrators sets national standards for health records and for methods of collecting and keeping them. Health record administrators have become involved in analysing the information and frequently appear in court to explain the system. Whether a patient has received average, reasonable and prudent care may, and will increasingly, depend on whether the appropriate standards have been met in recording the information upon which the patient's treatment was based. The health record administrator is increasingly at the centre of this information network.

With the increased number of personnel, services, disciplines and equipment involved in the care and treatment of patients, communication among all of the various parts is essential. The patient has a right to that communication taking place so as to avoid reasonably foreseeable injury.

The primary reason for having records, then, is to be able to coordinate the work of those involved in providing health care. It is also to record the information so that decisions regarding further care and treatment can be based on recorded fact and not on someone's memory.

The information must be in a format that everyone on the team understands and can use for the benefit of the patient. The format is not designed to communicate the information to the patient. Although information must be communicated to the patient, the patient record is not the means by which that communication takes place.

The Patient's Right to Reasonable Records

The patient's right to average, reasonable and prudent standards in the receipt of health care and treatment can be applied to patient records. The collection of information on the patient's condition, what was done for the patient and what the patient's reaction was is an integral part of the care and treatment of the patient. Without this information, medical, nursing and other decisions cannot be made in an informed and accurate manner. All health care decisions are based on information on the patient's history and current condition.

The actual medical procedure may be beyond reproach but may have injured the patient because a certain aspect of the patient's condition was not taken into consideration. The decision to give the patient a particular drug may have been the usual and proper course, but with the knowledge that the patient was allergic to that drug, following that course would cause injury, would be unreasonable and therefore would be negligence, for which the patient has the right to compensation. The patient may have been injured because a drug was given that interacted adversely with another drug the patient was taking. The person prescribing the drug must be aware of the other drugs currently being taken. This information is supposed to come from the patient's record.

The patient's right to a proper standard of care can therefore be breached because of various efforts involving health information. There may have been a failure on the part of a physician or a nurse to collect the information. If it is the ordinary practice to collect and record this information, since without it the patient could be injured, the failure to collect the information either by asking the patient or by diagnostic tests is negligence. Or the information may have been collected but not recorded. Those reading the record are entitled to assume that the ordinary course of seeking this information was followed. Because there is no record, the assumption is that there was no problem.

The information may have been collected but improperly, resulting in errors. This, too, would be considered negligence, since the patient has the right to have information collected accurately.

The information may have been collected properly but recorded improperly. A physician in prescribing may have confused the names of drugs, or the dosage may have been confused by mixing up numbers or confusing a zero for a decimal. Following such an erroneous order may not be negligent unless it should have been obvious that an error was made. The negligence would have been in the recording of the information.

Hospitals have a particular problem in recording information. Most of the people making entries in what is known as the chart, which is the patient's file or record, never see each other and may not even know each other. They work in many different disciplines, from medicine to nursing to inhalation therapy to social work, and in different departments of the hospital. The primary way they communicate with one another about a patient's condition, what was done for a patient and what the patient's reaction was is through the chart.

Entries are usually hand-written, which means that often records are difficult to read and incorrect readings may be made, resulting in action that is incorrect or even dangerous. Abbreviations may be used that the person reading does not understand, or terminology may differ from department to department and from person to person. Many institutions do not even use uniform abbreviations throughout the facility. The health care industry as a whole does not even use uniform abbreviations.

Furthermore, Canadian medical schools do not as a rule teach students how to record information on the chart, even though errors could jeopardize patient lives. Students are expected to learn during their hospital training, either as ward clerks or as interns.

Communication can be difficult, yet it must all come together in order to promote the health and safety of the patient. The patient has a legal right to that. Yet the patient has no way of making certain that that actually happens, except by a lawsuit after an injury occurs because of someone's negligence.

The standards of care to which the patient has a legal right involve a number of ways the patient record is used. If someone reading an entry does not understand it, but guesses, acts accordingly and injures the patient, that is negligence. If a pharmacist on reading the doctor's prescription notes that the drug will interact adversely with another drug the patient is taking, the patient has a right to have that pharmacist refuse to fill the prescription and seek the advice of the physician. The pharmacist cannot ignore the physician's order, nor can it be changed without consulting the physician.

To improve the system, hospitals and someday all health facilities will maintain all patient information on computer, and the file will be linked with doctors' offices, laboratories, pharmacies, hospitals and various clinics. This would improve the method and style of communication, since it would produce a uniform style and remove the problem of legibility. However, it would not prevent incorrect information being placed on the record, which may not be as easily noticed as it would be in a physical record. Even this, however, might be corrected if the computer was programmed to note that a particular dosage was improper for the circumstances. Unfortunately, such a program would not take into account medical judgement designed to meet the extraordinary needs of the patient. Developments are certainly taking place in the field of computerizing patient records, though a paperless record system is a very long way off.

Negligence can also take place in the use of the patient record. The most obvious case is the failure of a doctor to read the record before treating or advising the patient. This failure is clearly negligence if a patient is injured as a result.

The 1993 Quebec case of *Suite v. Cooke* dealt with a woman who had a non-therapeutic tubal ligation. Tissue samples were sent to the hospital pathology laboratory for analysis. A report was received by the hospital and the doctor revealing that a vein rather than the left fallopian tube had been ligated and that, therefore, the patient was not sterile.

There was no negligence in the manner in which the surgery was performed, since there is no guarantee of success in operations of this sort. However, the report was placed in the patient's file, and the doctor did not read it. About ten months later the patient consulted the doctor because her menstrual cycle had stopped. Only then did he read the report and find that the operation was not successful. In fact she was pregnant and later gave birth.

The court found that the doctor was negligent in not reading the report. If he had, he would have been able to advise the patient of her unsuccessful surgery and she would have been able to use other means to prevent conception. He would have known that by not telling her, the reasonably foreseeable result would be that she would assume that it was successful, do nothing, and possibly become pregnant. This is what happened, and she and her husband sued for "wrongful birth." They won the case and received compensation to help defray the costs. The husband was also compensated for loss of consortium during the latter stages of his wife's pregnancy and for psychological suffering.

Negligence can also occur if the record is incorrectly read. The reader arrives at an incorrect conclusion, takes action on the basis of that conclusion and injures the patient.

There is very little a patient can do to prevent such occurrences. The only recommendations that can be made are the following:

1. In providing a doctor with background information, the patient should provide as much as possible and make certain that it is accurate. The patient should not assume that certain conditions exist because of what seems to linger in the memory. The patient should advise the doctor to check on the accuracy of the information.

2. If a doctor does not advise the patient of the results of surgery or diagnostic tests, the patient should not assume that everything is

well. The patient should specifically ask for the results and expect a clear and definite answer.

3. The patient should prepare a list of the drugs currently being taken, giving the name, amount and frequency as well as the purpose. Presenting a copy of the list on admission to the hospital at least assists in preparing accurate records of current drug use. However, it is extremely important that the list is kept up to date, since if a hospital relies on an outdated list, serious injuries could result. The same practice should be followed when going to a new physician or dentist. Both prescription and non-prescription drugs should be on the list.

Does the Patient Own the Record?

Patients often assume that they own "their" records. They feel that since they indirectly paid for the health service, including the records, through government health insurance, the records belong to them. This applies particularly in dental offices, where patients are directly billed for x-rays that are part of the record. They therefore assume that they can demand them and take them away. This is not the case.

The records are the property of the person or institution that compiled them, not of the patient. What the patient has paid for, or what has been paid for on behalf of the patient, is not the record. It is the service that has been provided for the patient. This means that the patient does not have a legal right to take away the records. This is quite a different issue from whether the patient can have access to the records — to see them and to make copies of them.

Patient records must be kept for legal defence. In case the patient sues the doctor or the institution, evidence is required to defend the allegations. The records are a far more accurate source of details of what happened than the memories of any member of the staff.

Records are also collected for the purpose of research, for teaching, to support insurance payments and for numerous other reasons. An institution that would allow records to leave its possession would not be able to fulfil the reasons for which the records are compiled.

Even though the information is *about* the patient, it is not *for* the patient. It is, however, for the benefit of the patient, but as a communication it is directed towards other health professionals and not to the patient.

The result of this principle is that a patient does not have the right to demand the records. In fact, an institution or health care provider is quite unlikely to give away the records even if the care and treatment is complete.

The Patient's Access to Records

The traditional practice of hospitals and health care institutions generally was that patients were not permitted to see "their" records. The reasons were numerous. Patients would not understand them, since they were written in medical jargon. Patients might be misled because they might read them out of context. Finally, as one hospital complained, letting patients see records might lead to patient fishing expeditions that would provoke frivolous lawsuits.

As attitudes in the health care field changed, many hospitals continued to refuse patients access to records. However, when a lawyer for a patient sought access, it was invariably granted. Hospitals did not seem to realize that lawyers are merely hired guns for their clients.

The problem that has emerged in the past few years is that so many people and their lawyers are seeking access to their records and copies of them that health record departments are overburdened. It is often a time-consuming and expensive operation to assemble records, particularly if they are not all in the same place. As a result, many hospitals now charge a fee for access and copies. The argument is whether this fee in fact prevents a patient from having access.

It has always been clear that a patient and the lawyer representing the patient can have access on the order of a court. This may be obtained by starting a lawsuit. However, there have been instances of hospital foot-dragging resulting in additional costs to the plaintiff. An order can be obtained without a lawsuit.

Most enlightened institutions realize that responding quickly to a patient's request for records often diffuses the possibility of a suit or results in a smaller out-of-court settlement than if the request had been denied.

The answer for patients who want access is to retain a lawyer who is familiar with the workings of the health care field, and particularly with how record keeping takes place. The lawyer should be persistent but reasonable.

As with everything else, there are exceptions. The major exception falls within mental health legislation. Most provincial mental health laws permit psychiatric facilities to refuse patients access to records if it is felt that access to this information would be detrimental to the patient. There usually is an appeal provision. Because the process of appeal invariably involves a court, the patient should retain legal counsel when access has been refused.

Because access to records is easier than ever before, many health professionals, particularly in the psychiatric field, are concerned that information that could be detrimental to the patient or could upset the patient might be made available. As a result, some psychiatrists and psychologists are in the habit of keeping private notes, which are not entered in the official record. No mention is made of these notes, and the patient may never be aware of their existence. The only way to gain access to them is to start a lawsuit and obtain a court order for any records that might exist both inside and outside of the institution that are in the possession of the defendant. Failure to make the records available could result in the possessor being held in contempt of court. It is necessary to have proof that the defendant actually had the records, and refused to turn them over, despite the court order. All of this costs money.

Is There a Right to Confidentiality?

Confidentiality is relative. It really only exists in a society of one. One assumes that on going to a doctor, the intimate details of one's medical condition will not be broadcast at the next cocktail party. However, on entering hospital, it is obvious that a great number of people are going to learn the intimate details of one's condition. Patients do not ordinarily think of the vast number of people who will learn at least some of their personal information. How much they learn and whether it is necessary for all of these people to learn what they learn is a question well worth asking. The problem is to determine who should know what about the patient and how much they should know.

From a strictly legal point of view, there has always been some doubt about whether a patient in fact had a legal right to have personal information kept confidential. There are legislative provisions, especially in medicare statutes and various provincial hospital acts. Even without such legislation, it has always been assumed that patient information in a doctor's office or any health institution is confidential. The release of this information may impose liability if the patient were to sue. However, people usually do not sue, and in fact there have not been many court cases in Canada where patients have sued doctors or hospitals for releasing their confidential medical information. Because of the costs, and the uncertainty of whether there is a legal right, it usually is not worth doing.

Information about a patient is, of course, in the patient's record or chart. It is passed through the system by requisitions and consultative and diagnostic reports. Information may be transmitted at various medical staff and nursing meetings. As long as the information is passed along for the purpose of caring for or treating the patient, there is little basis for complaint.

There are a number of problem areas, though. The most common is that of idle chatter among doctors, nurses and others in hallways, elevators and cafeterias within hearing of other staff members not involved with the patient and of visitors.

Despite the persistent efforts of the Canadian Health Record Association, it is impossible to guarantee that someone in a staff of hundreds or even thousands will not blurt out inappropriate information about patients at the wrong time in the wrong place.

Some patients feel that even their presence in a hospital is confidential and should not be released to anyone. This is particularly true in psychiatric hospitals or psychiatric departments of general hospitals. As a result, some hospitals will not even acknowledge to callers that they have a particular patient. This may well antagonize family and friends who know very well that the patient is there. Administratively, it is difficult to set policies that will control the amount of information provided over the telephone or in person to someone who is asking about their Aunt Becky. Many hospitals do have policies that attempt to protect the amount of information released, though whether the patient has a legal right to be protected is a matter that has not been tested in the courts.

The second problem involves the teaching hospital, where medical, nursing and other students become involved with the patient not to treat or care for the patient but solely to use the patient as a "teaching tool." There is no doubt that patients provide excellent teaching "material." The issue is whether they have to submit to this, or even have the right to have their presence in the hospital and their private information kept from students.

It is often argued by the hospital administration that when a patient enters a teaching hospital, there is an implied consent to become part of the teaching process. Most patients do not have a choice of hospitals. The hospital would be in a difficult position if it attempted to deny admission or treatment on the grounds that the patient did not want to be seen by students unless they were involved in treatment.

A very persistent patient can usually ward off students from being part of the treatment team. However, it may be rather difficult to prevent students from prying into records, since they come as part of the hospital package.

As with everything else, there are definite exceptions to any right to have patient information kept confidential. The first is legislation. Every province and territory has legislation that requires hospitals and doctors to divulge certain patient information to public authorities. Births, deaths and stillbirths must be reported. Suspected child abuse must be reported, and in some provinces, suspected elder abuse or abuse of adults. Motor vehicle legislation often requires doctors to report cases of patients who suffer from any condition that makes it dangerous to drive a motor vehicle. Legislation governing coroners and medical examiners often requires them to report a case of death by suspected violence, negligence, misconduct or malpractice of another person. Workers compensation acts may also require that accidents be reported, with details of injuries.

Another exception arose in the 1976 case of *Tarasoff v. University of California*, which is quoted widely throughout the common law world. Although it has not been tested in Canadian courts, the principles upon which it was based apply also in Canada. In this case a student told his psychologist that he intended to kill a fellow student. He did just that. The family of the victim claimed that the victim had had a right to be warned. This of course would have meant that their right would overrule the right of the psychologist's patient to confidentiality. The Supreme Court of California agreed with the family. There is reason to believe that Canadian courts would take the same route.

Even when a patient is not likely to do danger to another person, private medical information may be divulged. If a patient arrives in the emergency department of a hospital with an injury that may have arisen from a criminal act, such as a gunshot or knife wound, legal writers have assumed that there is a higher public duty on the part of the hospital to call the police. However, the police have no right to see the records or obtain any information about a patient unless they are authorized by a warrant or court order. The mere arrival of a police officer in a doctor's office or a hospital health record department does not overcome the patient's right to confidentiality.

Various health facilities and professionals are often placed in a dilemma when a patient such as a pupil is referred for care. The question is whether the results of the treatment or care are to be reported back to the school so that the school can do whatever is necessary for the benefit of the child. The general legal opinion is that although the school may have referred the student, it is not acting on behalf of the student and therefore is not entitled to any information. The child and the child's parents have a right to the information being kept confidential.

Because of the close connections between many health, social service and education agencies, the free flow of health information is quite common. To overcome the problem of confidentiality, potential patients or their parents will frequently be asked to give up their right to confidentiality so that information can be released.

Correcting Errors in the Record
A situation occasionally arises, particularly in mental health facilities, where patients after gaining access to their records object to certain

entries. The objection may be to social or psychological background information that the patient says is incorrect, or to entries dealing with situations when the patient was undergoing care.

There is no legal right on the part of the patient to have the record changed. It is a record of information that was correctly collected, not necessarily a record of correct information. In some cases it is a record of information that one person who recorded it was told. The presumption is that it is correct, in that this information was in fact given to the recorder, not that the information itself was correct.

Unfortunately, if the information was incorrect, diagnoses and treatment based on it may also be incorrect, and the record could affect treatment and care for years to come. The patient should put in writing the information believed to be correct and send it to the hospital or agency or office, asking that it be added to the record and pointing out that the information in the record is incorrect. In this way, anyone reviewing the chart will be able to take the new information into consideration.

Defamation in the Record
Defamation is a written or spoken statement that is untrue and harmful to a person's reputation in the community. This definition can be applied generally across Canada, even though some provinces have legislation dealing with the subject whereas others maintain the traditional English common law distinction between libel (written defamation) and slander (spoken defamation). Quebec deals with the subject in its Civil Code.

There are two potential assaults on patient's rights arising out of what someone might consider a defamatory remark in the record.

The first potentially defamatory statement would be related to a diagnosis of an illness that would affect the person's reputation, such as a sexually transmitted disease or a mental illness. If the patient does have the disease mentioned, the statement is true and is not defamatory, even if it does harm the person's reputation. If the statement in the record is not true, the question then is whether the patient can sue for defamation.

It would be extremely difficult to sue a doctor, nurse, psychologist, social worker or any other person who made an entry in the records that is considered defamatory. Even if the statement was incorrect, the person making the entry is to a certain extent protected. As long as the entry was made without malice and in the belief that it was true, the courts would say that it was permissible to make it. Furthermore, the duty of the health professional is to record information *and opinion* that is necessary for the care and treatment of the patient. If the information that is recorded can be said to assist in care and treatment, the provider of the care is protected, even if the information or the opinion is found to be incorrect.

If, however, it could be shown that the information was not necessary for the care and treatment, this privilege may not apply.

A further complication arises if the statement does not deal with the patient at all but with some other person, such as a friend or relative of the patient. This might arise, for example, when a social worker is recording the life history of the patient and notes that when the patient was a child she was sexually abused by a particular individual. The question then is whether that individual could sue for defamation. As with any defamation suit, it would have to be shown that the statement made was incorrect. Once again, the defence would be the same. The defendant would be able to escape liability by showing that there was no malice and that the information was recorded in the belief that it was true and was required to fulfil the duty to care and treat the patient.

Computerization and the Future

Despite the practical difficulties and the financial restraints, more and more of a patient's health information is placed on a computer. With computerization, the health care system can more easily move towards linking all medical records. Such a system has both positive and negative features.

On the positive side, it means that if a patient enters an emergency department in Winnipeg, the hospital can immediately determine that the patient has had certain operations in Halifax and Toronto and has had certain medical conditions diagnosed by various doctors in various places. Through links with pharmacies, the hospital would also know what drugs the patient is taking. As a result, an immediate and accurate picture of the patient's condition would be available, thus assisting in making a diagnosis without the usual guesswork. The possibility of drug interactions can be lessened, since everyone will know what drugs the patient is currently taking and avoid prescribing something to which the patient is allergic. It will also result in the availability of fast transcontinental and international consultations on the basis of information sent quickly and accurately from place to place.

The difficulties, however, are numerous. Errors in the information will be compounded and everyone treating the patient will rely on them. It may become more difficult to discover errors and to remove them.

There is also the problem of confidentiality. Once a patient's information is on computer and part of a medical record linkage system, there is always the danger that people who are not involved in treating the patient will have access to it and can take action as a result of the information that may harm the patient. This may include insurance companies that may deny coverage, employers and the police. It may also include the government, which might attempt to use the fact that a patient has had psychiatric care for political purposes. Leaks to the press are also possible.

Various access codes will be required to lessen these dangers, and the consent of the patient will be required to permit access. Despite the best efforts, however, errors will occur and lives will be damaged. No system is foolproof, regardless of how technically advanced it may be or how many assurances politicians and civil servants give. The question is whether society is prepared to risk the price in order to have the benefits of a computerized health information linkage system.

Summary of Principles

1. The purpose of the patient record is to be able to coordinate and to record information gathered by one or more health professionals for the purpose of treating or caring for the patient.

2. The patient record is owned by the provider of the service, such as the hospital or private physician or dentist, and not by the patient.

3. The patient has a legal right to have the record compiled and used in an average, reasonable and prudent manner so as to provide treatment or care according to appropriate standards.

4. The patient ordinarily has a right to have access to the record and to make copies of the record, though in some instances, particularly involving psychiatric care, there may be some exceptions.

5. There is usually considered to be a right to have information collected by health providers kept confidential, though exceptions to this rule are outlined in various acts or by court order.

10

CAN A
DOCTOR HAVE
SEX WITH
A PATIENT?

I N 1978, LAURA NORBERG, a British Columbia teenager, was suffering from severe headaches and pain in her jaw. More and more painkillers were prescribed before the problem was diagnosed as an abscessed tooth. The tooth was removed and the pain ended, but Miss Norberg had become addicted to painkillers.

In 1981 she found Dr. Morris Wynrib, a physician in his seventies, who was willing to supply her with painkillers for pain she said was caused by a broken ankle earlier that year. Dr. Wynrib finally accused her of being addicted. She admitted her addiction. He in turn offered her more drugs in return for sexual relations.

She tried to obtain drugs from other doctors and to buy them illegally, but eventually her supply dried up and she returned to Dr. Wynrib. Up to 1985 they had ten to twelve encounters of simulated intercourse, after which he would give her the drugs. No physical force was used. She knew he was lonely and played on the fact that he liked her. She later sued Dr. Wynrib for sexual assault, negligence, breach of fiduciary duty and breach of contract.

When the case worked its way up to the Supreme Court of Canada in 1992, Norberg came out the winner: she won the grand total of $30,000.

No one suggests that every doctor, or for that matter dentist, psychologist or social worker, is getting into bed with patients. However, studies indicate that a sufficient number of them do it, or try to do it, or at least suggest it, that it is a matter of concern for the medical profession and the public. A significant number of cases go before provincial disciplinary bodies, and some of them end up in open court.

The cases that go to court do so for one of three reasons. One is that the patient sues the doctor, as in *Norberg v. Wynrib*. The second is that the patient has complained to a provincial disciplinary body and either the patient or the accused has appealed to the courts. The third is that a criminal prosecution has been launched by the Crown Prosecutor.

The issue of sexual harassment of patients is clear. It is considered unprofessional conduct, and the doctor or other professional can be disciplined. The Code of Ethics of the Canadian Medical Association clearly states that a physician will not take physical, emotional or financial advantage of the patient.

Forced sex is in a similar category, as well as being considered assault and battery for which the patient could sue. It is also an offence under the Criminal Code. In the case of a member of the medical staff of a hospital, it is grounds for immediate removal of hospital privileges. If the person is an employee of a hospital, long-term-care facility, clinic or home care agency, it is grounds for immediate dismissal.

However, in many of the cases that arise, the patient has consented to having sexual relations but later complains that the consent was not freely given.

The view taken by the medical profession and the courts is that a doctor and a patient are not equals. When a person consults a doctor and becomes a patient, that person is in need of that doctor's services and has little choice once the patient–provider relationship is established. For many purposes it may be seen as a simple contract, but psychologically the patient needs the doctor and is frequently dependent on the doctor for relief. For this reason, even if a patient consents to having sexual relations with a doctor, the legal and professional attitude is that the consent may not have been given freely. For this reason, physicians are virtually prohibited from having sexual relations with their patients.

These situations of course are not restricted to physicians. They apply to other health professionals, but especially to those on whom the patient is heavily dependent for care or treatment, such as a dentist, a psychologist or a nurse.

A problem arises when a physician treats a patient from time to time, which makes it difficult to determine whether the patient–provider relationship has ended when sexual relations take place. If it can be shown that further care or treatment may be required, it may be that the relationship, and therefore the dependency, has not ended. If this is the case, the physician is not permitted sexual relations with the patient.

There are also situations in which the patient initiates and even encourages sexual relations with a doctor. There are no legal restraints on a patient. However, the doctor is under an obligation to refuse these advances. If they persist, the doctor would be justified in ending the patient–provider relationship and referring the patient to another doctor, or at least advising the patient to seek services elsewhere.

The doctor who is faced with this situation is well advised to record all advances made by the patient in order to rebut any accusations that the patient may make at a later date.

A further problem that arises is that of treatment that may be considered sexual in nature. A patient has the right to be treated in a manner according to the standard practice in the profession and according to appropriate professional ethics. Therefore, sexual relations between a therapist and a patient in the guise of treatment are clearly unethical and fall into the same situation as in the *Norberg v. Wynrib* case. It is a breach of the professional's duty to the patient, and it is highly questionable whether the patient's consent is valid.

Sexual relations are not limited to intercourse. Touching the patient in a sexual manner may be just as damaging. The problem is that there may be some question about whether an act such as touching genitals or a vaginal examination is a medical or intended as a sexual act. This will depend on the facts of the individual case. There is no definition that can be applied to all situations.

To protect themselves against accusations of sexual assault, male physicians frequently have a female assistant or colleague present when examining a female patient. The patient who demands the right not to have company during such a procedure may be refused. The door of the examination room may be left open so that the patient who objects to what is occurring may cry out.

Most physicians are extremely careful in explaining what is to take place so that there will be no misunderstanding about the purpose of the procedure. This of course does not prevent close contact that may be interpreted as sexual. As long as the procedure is standard practice, however, it would be very difficult for a patient to prove that there were sexual overtones.

If a patient feels uncomfortable during a procedure, it is important for the patient to tell the person treating them that they feel uncomfortable and ask whether it is necessary. If over a series of appointments the patient continues to have similar feelings, an outside opinion of whether the procedure or the method is standard practice might be obtained. The patient should also consider changing to another health care provider. In a hospital or long-term-care facility, the patient should bring concerns to someone in authority, such as the director of nursing or the supervisor in the case of a home care agency.

Summary of Principles

1. Sexual relations between a patient and a health care professional while any semblance of dependency as part of a patient–provider relationship exists are forbidden by the disciplinary body of that profession.
2. The patient–provider relationship may continue to exist long after regular visits have ended, and during which sexual relations are prohibited.
3. A patient who has been subjected to sexual relations or sexual contact may complain to the disciplinary body of the profession concerned and consider legal action on the basis of assault, negligence or a breach of fiduciary duty.

11

HOSPITAL

INSURANCE

AND

MEDICARE

NOT SO MANY YEARS AGO Canada's health system was the envy
of the world. In most other countries, the delivery of health
care was a service like any other. Just like accounting services,
plumbing services or the services of a garage mechanic, the customer
had to pay. Complex schemes have been set up in many countries for
private and public insurance. Many countries developed a two-tiered
system of private hospitals for those who could afford to go there or
had private insurance to cover the costs, and public hospitals for
everyone else.

Canada took the moral high ground. It established a system
whereby services for the treatment of illness would be provided to all
Canadians, rich or poor, without any direct cost to them. Hospital
services and physician's services would be provided as freely and as
openly as the use of public parks, highways and schools. The philos-
ophy gradually developed that when a person's health is at stake, the

issue of money should not be considered. They should get treatment regardless of who they are or how much money they had. The result is that when a Canadian is discharged from a hospital, no bill is received, except for uninsured services such as the additional cost of a semi-private or private room or the cost of renting a television or a telephone. Consequently, patients have no idea what the services cost. As far as they are concerned, the services are "free," just like the CBC and the weather bureau.

There are many criticisms of this approach. None the less, it accomplished the goal of removing any worries about money when a person is sick. To Canadians, the American system and the systems of many other countries are crass, discriminatory and frankly immoral.

The system was funded to a large extent by the federal government but administered by provincial governments though over the years the provinces have assumed a greater burden of the financing. Some provinces raised their share of the costs through general revenue, whereas others charged premiums. There were also special programs for the military, federal prisoners, the RCMP and native Indians. Virtually everyone in the country was insured for almost all hospital and medical services.

After years of negotiations, patients from one province did not even have to make a claim against their province's health program when they received services elsewhere in Canada. When the hospital insurance program was initiated in the 1950s, various services were not insured, such as numerous out-patient services. Over the years the insured list became almost all-inclusive. Later, a medicare program was started for the cost of physicians' services. Subsequently, other programs were started in the provinces, with a gradual expansion of what was insured.

In addition, numerous other health services were "free" for some, or sometimes for all, residents, even though they were not technically part of the hospital insurance or medicare programs. (These programs also differed from province to province.) The popular attitude therefore arose that health service was a public service to which all Canadian *residents* (not necessarily citizens) had a right. Even though it was called insurance, it did not look like insurance, and therefore really was not. Unlike the standard deductible of most insurance policies, medical and hospital services were paid complete-ly. For many years, user fees have been prohibited.

In addition to the very broad benefits provided within Canada, the programs were worldwide, at least for emergencies and any pro-cedures that were medically necessary outside Canada. Canada was one of the few countries that offered its residents a worry-free inter-national environment when it came to the payment of health ser-vices. In the past number of years the extent of the benefits has become so narrow that Canadian residents receiving treatment out-side the country are not really protected to any great degree.

What made the Canadian system so unique was that, despite the accusations of right-wing Americans, it was not "socialized" medicine. Government did not provide the services. The institu-tions and people who had provided health care before health insur-ance continued to do so. The system of giving care remained the same, and in fact remains not that different from the system in the United States. Patients choose their own physician, dentist (where some dental services are insured) or pharmacy (where pharmaceuti-cal services are covered). Patients choose their own hospital (assum-ing their physician has privileges to admit them to that hospital). In the United States, patients insured under an HMO (Health Maintenance Organization) do not have the same freedom of choice.

The health insurance schemes are established by an act of each province. The legal rights of patients are those given to them under this legislation. The rights established under the legislation do not guarantee the right to actually receive the service listed. They guaran-tee that the services will be paid for by the provincial health plan. There are two restrictions.

For services in Canada, the rate of payment is the full amount at the basic ward rate. This rate includes all in-patient services, whereas in the United States and many other countries, the ward rate includes only the bed, basic nursing care and meals.

The second major restriction is on the amounts that are paid for services rendered outside Canada. Invariably, the charges are signifi-cantly higher elsewhere, which means that the Canadian health insurance plans will not nearly cover the amount charged.

The most profound effect on patients and their rights under the health insurance programs results from the current financial state of the country. This has made the health insurance programs — and the entire health system — a shambles.

The cause has been, to a large extent, a naive population led on by incompetent politicians greedy for votes. The initial idea of health insurance was commendable, but because it insured only the most expensive services, it resulted in the use of those services rather than services that were just as effective and cheaper. Patients languished in Canadian hospitals when full-scale hospital services were not necessary. These patients may have been better served in long-term-care facilities or even in home care, but neither was insured.

Small community hospitals were kept open for years after they were no longer needed in order to satisfy the desires of communities and the prestige of local boards. Hospitals were penalized when they saved money, by having their budgets cut the following year. Regional centres were established for various procedures in order to attract stellar medical staff when it would have been cheaper and better to transport patients to large centres of expertise.

The result is that the system is collapsing. The result for patients has often been sloppy care from demoralized staff and physicians as budgets are cut and supplies and facilities diminish.

For many procedures there are now lengthy waiting lists. Even though the risks of waiting may be low, it often means that patients are virtually out of commission until their treatment takes place. Their income and productivity drop, and they may be a burden on their families. The cost of this is never considered.

Many patients go to the United States where, if funds are available, the procedure can take place almost immediately. Nothing prevents Canadians from taking advantage of some of the best centres in the world south of the border. However, most provincial plans will not cover any of the costs on the grounds that the procedure is available in Canada. It is true that the procedure is available. But it is not available when the patient requires it.

Although Canadian physicians admit that a patient may require the surgery now, they also say that the risk of waiting is small.

Governments interpret this to mean that to go outside the country would solely be for the patient's convenience.

This does not prevent Canadians from travelling outside Canada to receive hospital services at their own cost. In the long run, they may find that it is not as expensive as they imagined, since much of the cost will be a personal tax deduction.

Canadians who want to pay for their treatment outside Canada should be careful to shop around for price and quality. The United States, for instance, may have not only some of the finest health services in the Western world but also some of the poorest. There is also the danger in the United States of patients being over-treated because of the need of hospitals to increase their income. This is also a country where hospitals advertise.

Overall, though, the opportunities to go outside the hospital insurance program in Canada are strictly limited. They tend to be mainly for out-patient services, depending on the province. Physiotherapy services from a private clinic may be more readily accessible than those offered in a hospital, except that in a clinic the patient must pay. The same is not true for some sophisticated diagnostic services or in-patient services that are generally not available in Canada outside the hospital insurance programs. This means that a patient cannot choose to go to a private hospital or have a private bed in a public hospital and pay the cost personally. With the financial straits the Canadian health system finds itself facing, this may become a possibility in the future.

Summary of Principles
1. The right of all residents of Canada to insured services under the health insurance program is not a right to those services; it is a right to have those services paid for at the rates set by the provincial program.
2. The right of patients to services differs from province to province even though the basic coverage is the same throughout the country.
3. Non-emergency services outside the country may be insured only if prior permission is granted.

12

DRUG

STORES

THE LEGAL RELATIONSHIP BETWEEN the patient and the pharmacy, or more particularly the pharmacist, has changed in the past few years. In the past, the patient received a prescription from a doctor, which authorized the pharmacist to dispense the drug and to sell it to the patient. For those drugs for which the law did not require a prescription, the pharmacist was at liberty to sell whatever the patient wanted to buy. However, the growing sophistication of pharmacies has begun to change this simple arrangement.

It is now recognized that not all physicians are as knowledgeable as they ought to be about the properties of the drugs they prescribe. They do not have the time or the resources to determine whether a particular dosage is appropriate given the patient's condition, and may not be aware of the possibilities of the drug interacting with other drugs the patient is taking.

Pharmacists are supposed to be experts in the use of drugs and their interactions. Therefore, to a greater and greater extent pharmacists are becoming the watchdog of physicans' prescribing practices. In many hospitals, clinical pharmacists make rounds and are required to assist in determining the appropriate medication for patients.

Therefore, if a physician prescribes a drug that is inappropriate for a patient or that interacts with the patient's current medications, the pharmacist has a duty to the patient to contact the physician to discuss the matter and to work out a solution. It may be appropriate in the physician's judgement to prescribe a drug that ordinarily would be inappropriate but because of particular conditions is appropriate for this patient. Given such an explanation, the pharmacist may proceed. However, there may be situations in which it is never appropriate to prescribe such a drug to such a patient. In this case, the matter should be referred to the pharmacy licensing body for discussion with the medical licensing authorities, so that a solution may be found.

The pharmacist also has a duty to obtain an explanation for any drug that may interact with the patient's current medications. It may be that the physician was not aware that the patient was taking certain other drugs. This system, however, works to the benefit of the patient only if the pharmacist knows all the drugs being taken by the patient. If the patient deals with more than one pharmacist, or more than one doctor, it becomes difficult for a pharmacist to provide this service. Furthermore, the patient cannot expect this service and would not have a right to it.

It may be argued that before dispensing any medication, a pharmacist should ask all patients what other drugs they are taking, or at least warn them about taking certain other medications that could cause a drug interaction. The defence would be that the pharmacist is entitled to rely on the prescribing physician to not prescribe drugs that might interact. The same could be true of drugs to which the patient may be allergic. Pharmacists already advise patients about taking drugs, such as with plenty of water, or not with alcohol.

Because of the uncertainties of this relationship, it would be difficult to determine how far the patient's rights extend. If, however, the pharmacist has complete control over the patient's medications, the patient's rights are much more extensive, since the patient has the right to expect the pharmacist to assess the entire drug profile and to intervene if necessary.

If a prescription is unclear, either because it is illegible or because the instructions are not clear, the pharmacist has a duty to clarify the prescription, and the patient has a right to have the pharmacist do so. The pharmacist cannot guess and dispense the drug. Contact must be made with the physician to make certain that the prescription is correct.

With the growing implementation of computer-linked patient records providing pharmacists with ever-increasing amounts of personal information on patients, the duty of the pharmacist to the patient will grow. Patients who are injured because of prescribed medications will allege pharmaceutical negligence on the grounds that the pharmacist knew, or ought to have known, that the action taken would cause, or could reasonably have caused, the injury that did in fact occur.

Summary of Principles
1. The patient has a right to receive from the pharmacist a standard of care equal to that of the average, reasonable and prudent pharmacist in the circumstances.
2. The pharmacist has a duty to the patient to prevent inappropriate drugs and drug interactions insofar as this duty can reasonably be expected of a pharmacist.

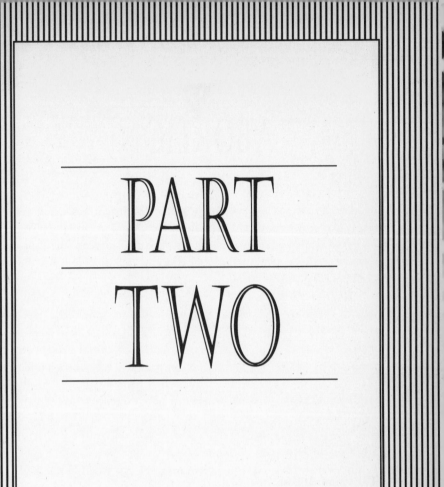

PART
TWO

13

ABORTION

The Criminal Past

NO MATTER WHAT Parliament or any provincial legislature does, no matter what the courts do, the debate over abortion continues unabated. Abortion continues to get press coverage and continues to be the focus of public demonstrations and attempts to change the law. This is certainly not unique in Canada. Countries all over the world are engaged in this struggle.

The Canadian situation until a few years ago was centred on a debate over the Criminal Code. Abortion was the only medical procedure specifically mentioned in Canada's criminal law, which simply forbade abortion unless it could be shown that the procedure was necessary to save the life of the mother.

Quite understandably, physicians who wanted to perform abortions were nervous about doing so, because they would not know until afterwards whether they had in fact met the provisions of the law. They would have to be charged with a criminal offence and then hope that they would be found not guilty.

In 1969, Parliament set down a procedure that would sanction an abortion before it was performed, and at least in that one instance decriminalize it. This procedure allowed, but did not require, certain hospitals to set up therapeutic abortion committees, which would determine whether the pregnancy would endanger, or would be likely to endanger, the life or health of the mother. If the committee decided that it would, a certificate to this effect was given that permitted the doctor to perform the abortion and the mother to have it done. The abortion had to be performed in a hospital that was accredited or approved.

This provision permitted a wide divergence of practice across the country. Many hospitals disapproved of abortions and therefore did not set up committees, so that no certificates were granted. Others set up committees that were so liberal in their interpretation of the words "life or health" that almost everyone who asked for a certificate got one.

The procedure did not create a legal right to an abortion. It should be remembered that there is no unqualified right to any other elective procedure, either.

It also restricted a woman in having an abortion performed outside a hospital in a clinic, unless the clinic was authorized as a hospital for the purposes of performing abortions by the provincial minister of health.

Finally, after a series of cases involving Dr. Henry Morgentaler, who promoted abortions for women who wanted them, the Supreme Court of Canada decided that the provisions of the Criminal Code placing various legal hurdles in front of a woman seeking an abortion were unconstitutional and therefore invalid. They infringed on a woman's right to fundamental justice under the Canadian Charter of Rights and Freedoms.

Rather than trying to correct the legal deficiencies, the federal government did nothing. At the present time, therefore, there is no criminal legislation specifically dealing with the termination of pregnancy, just as there is no criminal legislation dealing specifically with any other medical or surgical procedure. The result is that hospitals may perform abortions without any reference to the Criminal Code of Canada. They do not *have* to perform abortions, however.

This does not mean that women have gained the legal right to an abortion. It means that an abortion is not a criminal act by itself. It also does not mean that criminal charges cannot arise out of an abortion, solely because it is an abortion. They can, but in the same way that many other activities could be regarded as criminal under certain circumstances.

A conviction for criminal negligence could arise if an abortion was performed with such "wanton or reckless disregard" for the life or safety of the woman that injury or death resulted. An abortion performed on a woman against her will could constitute a number of crimes, including aggravated assault. The actions upon which these criminal charges are laid may also provoke a civil lawsuit brought by the woman for compensation.

It has been thought over the years that many abortions were performed not by physicians but by others in non-medical facilities. The Criminal Code does not specifically deal with these "back-street" abortions. However, the performance of an abortion is clearly a medical act reserved solely for the medical profession. Anyone who is not licensed to practise medicine in a particular province or territory in Canada would be in breach of the provincial or territorial medical legislation and could be convicted.

A Woman's Rights

It is clear that no woman has a legal right to an abortion as a matter of principle. However, if a physician found that a pregnancy clearly would endanger the life or health of the woman but would not terminate the pregnancy, it might be speculated that the woman then has a legal right to an abortion.

What a woman does have is the basic right — which every patient has — to average, reasonable and prudent care when an abortion is performed. Failure to abide by this standard that results in injury to the woman is negligence, for which the mother can be compensated. (See chapter 5, "Negligence and Standards of Care.")

The Supreme Court of British Columbia was faced with this issue in the 1990 case of *Cherry v. Borsman*. In 1982, Jody Cherry learned that she was pregnant and decided to undergo a therapeutic abortion. The procedure took place at ten and a half weeks gestation, and the pathology report indicated the presence of only immature placental tissue. Because she continued to bleed for three weeks, her family physician suspected that she was still pregnant. The physician who performed the abortion disagreed. Finally, an ultrasound determined that she was carrying a foetus of between nineteen and twenty-six weeks gestation in the breech position. Ms. Cherry went into premature labour, and the baby was born at thirty-one weeks. The child was left with cerebral palsy, mental retardation, serious motor handicaps and incontinence.

Ms. Cherry sued for negligence and won. The court found that the defendant, Dr. Borsman, had provided substandard care by miscalculating gestation and by not taking proper measures to ensure the removal of foetal tissue during the abortion. Furthermore, the court found that the child's injuries were a result of the negligent abortion, but that an alternative theory of liability also could be based on "wrongful birth": as a result of the negligent abortion, a mother may seek compensation for any expenses as a result of undergoing the unwanted pregnancy. She will not, however, be awarded compensation to bring up the child.

The question also arises whether Canadian courts will accept a lawsuit brought by a child who was born because of a negligently performed abortion. Canadian courts will not accept wrongful-life suits, since such a suit implies that someone should be compensated for being alive. If, however, the child was injured as a result of the physician's negligence, it would be possible for the child to sue for those injuries quite apart from being born.

Because of the Supreme Court of Canada ruling striking down the Criminal Code provision on abortion, Canadian women have more choice in where the procedure may be performed. No longer is a woman restricted to a hospital abortion, she may go to other facilities. As with other private facilities, though, there is no duty on the part of the facility to accept the woman as a patient, nor on the part of any doctor to take on an abortion regardless of the reason.

It would appear that an abortion for a female under the age of majority or having some mental disability is to be treated no differently then any other medical or surgical treatment on women in these circumstances.

A Father's Rights

During the debate over abortion, the issue arose of whether the father of the foetus has any legal rights. Since various legal duties will be placed on the father if the child is born, the question is whether the father has any rights over whether it will be born.

The first question is whether the father can prevent the mother from having an abortion. This matter was dealt with by the Supreme Court of Canada in the case of *Tremblay v. Daigle,* reported in the law reports in 1989. The court issued a clear statement that the father had no right to veto a woman's decision with respect to the foetus. Therefore, the father does not have to be asked for permission. The matter of an abortion is solely within the discretion of the woman.

Similarly, the father has no legal right to require the woman to have an abortion when she does not want it, even if he assisted in the creation of the child and will bear legal obligations towards it on its birth.

The law with respect to abortions has completely emancipated women in making decisions about their own bodies, which includes, until birth, the bodies of their unborn babies.

A Doctor's Rights

Nothing requires a doctor to perform an abortion, unless there is a continuing duty to care for a patient who, as a matter of reasonable care, requires termination of the pregnancy. However, a doctor who will not do abortions for whatever reason may be under a legal duty to advise the patient of this and to refer the patient to someone who will, or at least give the patient the opportunity to seek medical assistance elsewhere.

The patient has a right not to be abandoned. The physician cannot be in the midst of treating a patient and then refuse to carry out a procedure that is medically necessary. Similarly, a physician cannot receive a patient for the purpose of performing an abortion and then refuse to continue after the procedure has begun.

Summary of Principles

1. Abortions in Canada are no longer criminal acts and therefore are treated the same as all other medical procedures.

2. No woman has an absolute right to an abortion unless it is medically necessary in the same way as any other medically necessary procedure that requires hospital admission.

3. No doctor has a legal duty to perform abortions but cannot abandon a patient who requires one or on whom the doctor has already commenced the procedure.

4. The matter of consent to an abortion is solely within the discretion of the woman. The father of the foetus has no right either to require the woman to have an abortion or to prevent her from having it.

5. The woman undergoing an abortion has the legal right to have it performed according to average, reasonable and prudent standards, just like any other medical or surgical procedure.

14

STERILIZATION

THERE IS SOMETHING FRIGHTENING about sterilization. Regardless of what we might think about family planning, the procedure does seem to remove what our culture tells us is one of our purposes in life, to have children and perpetuate the human race. Our culture has also taught us that the ability to "make" babies is one thing that makes us "men" or "women." Without that ability we are not complete. It is not surprising, therefore, that lawsuits have arisen regarding medical sterilization.

Consent to Sterilization
As with every other medical or surgical procedure, the patient must consent to sterilization. (See chapter 4, "Consent to Treatment.") Just as with all other procedures, the patient's consent is valid only if it is fully informed. The patient has a right to be informed of the nature, risks and benefits of the procedure, any reasonable alterna-

tives and any risks and benefits of not undergoing the procedure. The patient must be given all information that the average person would want to know in order to make a decision.

The decision for sterilization is made by the patient alone, not by the physician or surgeon. It does not matter whether the sterilization is to be performed on a male or a female, or whether the patient is married or unmarried. The principles are the same. It does not matter whether the procedure is to be performed to prevent medical complications of pregnancy or whether it is purely for personal reasons.

The patient has the right to be informed specifically of two potential risks. The first is that the procedure either is not or may not be reversible. The second is that in many situations it is impossible to guarantee success. A man must be warned of the risk of impregnating his sexual partner for a certain time after a vasectomy while sperm is still present.

If a doctor does not want to perform the procedure for ethical or other reasons, the patient should be advised to see another doctor. A doctor may not wish to perform a vasectomy on an unmarried young male, for fear that the patient may change his mind later and want the procedure reversed.

Whether a patient requires the consent of the spouse used to be a difficult question. Because of the long history during which wives were largely under the control and "protection" of the husband, the practice in the health community was to obtain the husband's consent for sterilization of his wife, in addition to the wife's consent. However, since the husband was never under the protection of the wife, a husband could be sterilized without the consent of his wife, and even without her knowledge.

Some provinces, such as Quebec, specifically changed this requirement. However, even without changes in provincial law, the realization among lawyers and health care facilities was that a husband does not have any responsibility over the body of his wife. While there are responsibilities that go along with marriage, a husband does not have any responsibility over any medical or surgical care of his wife. She has sole control and therefore does not need his permission to obtain these services, even where these services affect the marital relationship between the couple, including their ability to produce children. It could be said that sterilization does affect that relationship.

The result is that the husband does not have to be asked for his consent to the sterilization of his wife. He should not be asked and cannot demand any right to be asked. The husband also has no legal right to prevent his wife from being sterilized.

Because historically a man was not under the protection of anyone and therefore had sole authority over his own body, these issues never arose when a man was to be sterilized. A wife did not have to consent to his sterilization and could not prevent it. Nothing has changed.

The law as it stands does not prevent any doctor from suggesting to either a husband or a wife that the proposed sterilization be discussed between them and that both should seek independent medical advice. Some doctors will not perform the procedure on a married person unless the spouse is consulted and receives medical advice, so that misunderstandings about the procedure do not develop.

As with all other procedures, consent can be given only by a person who is mentally competent to give consent and who has the legal capacity. If a person is not mentally or legally competent, the guardian or parent ordinarily has the authority to consent on the patient's behalf. However, the Supreme Court of Canada, in the case of *Re Eve*, would not allow the mother of a mentally retarded girl to consent to sterilization on her daughter's behalf because the court did not believe that the procedure was medically required. This decision was reached despite the evidence that the daughter would not understand intercourse or the risk of pregnancy and would not be able to cope with pregnancy. It was also stated that the daughter would not be able to cope with menstruation. Still, there was no therapeutic reason to carry out the procedure.

Negligent Sterilization

From time to time, sterilizations are performed in a negligent manner or the operation is unsuccessful and the patient is not told. The result is frequently a birth that is unexpected and unwanted. It may be argued that the mother should be required to have an abortion rather than give birth and then complain about it. However, there may be a number of religious or psychological factors preventing her from taking this action. The result is negligence resulting in either "wrongful birth" or "wrongful life."

Wrongful birth is the action taken by the mother in the event of unwanted pregnancy. If it can be proven that the doctor was negligent, the pregnancy and the delivery are the obvious "injuries" that have been suffered and for which the mother can claim compensation. Canadian courts draw the line at awarding compensation to the mother for the costs of bringing up the unwanted child, though logically if the pregnancy and the delivery are injuries, then raising the child is inevitable.

The father is also entitled to a certain amount of compensation for the wrongful birth. This would be not only for the worry involved but also for the loss of marital intercourse during at least part of the pregnancy.

Wrongful life is the action brought by a child claiming that as a result of the negligence of the doctor, his or her life was produced "wrongfully." The plaintiff seeks compensation for having been born. As strange as this may seem, one can well imagine the argument of a child who was born with a genetic disease that was predicted before birth. However, Canadian courts do not accept the idea of a lawsuit for wrongful life, as a matter of public policy.

No sterilization can be guaranteed, though in most cases the procedure may be almost 100 percent certain. If, however, the doctor did in fact guarantee success and the sterilization was not successful, the patient would be able to base a claim on breach of contract, since there was a contract that included a guarantee.

If no such guarantee existed and sterilization was not successful, this is not necessarily the result of surgical negligence. It may well be negligence to not do the appropriate tests to determine the success of the surgery or to not advise the patient that sterility did not occur. As a result of any of these actions, a child may be conceived and there may be a right to compensation for the pregnancy and delivery.

Negligence may also arise during surgery that might cause injury to the patient, as with any surgery. The patient may have sustained nerve damage, or have contracted a communicable disease during surgery, for example. Even though sterility resulted, the failure to follow appropriate standards of care may result in other injuries for which the patient has a right to compensation. (See chapter 5, "Negligence and Standards of Care.") The patient's right, therefore, is not to be restricted to the fact of sterilization.

Summary of Principles

1. The patient has a right to give a fully informed consent to any sterilization procedure, including the right to be informed of all of those matters to which the patient would be informed in any other procedure.

2. The patient has the right particularly to be informed of the chance of success or failure of the sterilization.

3. A married man or woman has the right to be sterilized without the consent of the spouse.

4. To consent to sterilization, the person must be mentally capable of consenting and have the legal capacity to do so.

5. The woman who becomes pregnant as a result of a negligent sterilization or negligent post-operative testing or advice has the right to be compensated for the wrongful birth.

6. The husband of a woman who has the right to be compensated for a wrongful birth also has the right to be compensated.

7. The child who is born as a result of a wrongful birth does not have the right in Canada to sue for wrongful life.

15

HAVING

A BABY

BY

TECHNOLOGY

THE WONDERFUL AND FRIGHTENING world of science fiction has arrived. Science and technology have arisen to serve the human race in perpetuating itself. Or, as some might say, the human race is serving the ends of science and technology, threatening the bonds of human relations, our religious and moral beliefs and traditions, and the law. Nowhere is this more striking than in the area of procreation.

The law and lawyers struggle to apply the law as it reflected the old way of human procreation to the new. The results are often unclear, causing fear and uncertainty among those who wish to make use of new scientific developments.

There is such concern that the federal government has spent more than $28 million on the Royal Commission on Reproductive Technology. How many of its recommendations will be translated into legislation remain to be seen. One of the main concerns of the commission is the lack of standards in the reproductive technology business and the fear that human life will be bought and sold as a commercial commodity.

It is in this area of scientific advance that traditional ethical values may be so widely held that law will be passed to enforce these values. A similar reaction has taken place in Europe, where women well past menopause have been artificially impregnated and are able to carry the foetus to term.

Assuming that there are no scientific or medical reasons to prevent such procedures, there are no legal implications other than those that have been traditionally raised in instances of artificial reproduction. The practices could be prevented only by the medical profession declaring them unethical, thus exposing any physician involved to disciplinary action, or by outlawing in legislation these procedures or any business arrangements involved.

The issue then would be whether such legislation would contravene the Canadian Charter of Rights and Freedoms, in particular the right to life, liberty and the security of the person. The Charter's opening section allows legislation to put a reasonable limit on rights and freedoms as can be demonstrably justified in a free and democratic society. The question then would be whether the legislation can be demonstrably justified. These are the questions that will no doubt challenge, shock and titillate Canadians over the next few years.

Artificial Insemination by the Husband (AIH)

One of the oldest methods of assisting couples who want children and have not been able to have them is artificial insemination. Semen is collected from a male donor and inserted into the female.

Insemination using the sperm of the husband is the most straightforward method and causes the fewest legal complications. It does not affect the relationship between the husband and the wife, since the husband is still the father and the wife is the mother. It also does not affect the relationship and the duties that each have towards any resulting child. Except for the method by which procreation took place, the circumstances are the same as would be the case if the method was natural intercourse.

Complications arise if the husband's sperm is frozen for later use, as may be done if the husband for one reason or another is expecting the possibility of losing the ability to impregnate his wife, such as through testicular surgery, and the husband subsequently dies. Certainly, the sperm can still be used by the widow. However, two issues arise.

If the sperm bank refuses to release the sperm to the widow, the first question is whether she has a legal right to it. There is no such right in legislation. However, if there is a contract between the sperm bank and the widow, or between the sperm bank and the late husband, there may be a right. Therefore, it is important that if a husband has his sperm frozen and preserved, this issue should be dealt with by contract one way or another.

It may be argued that sperm is an inherited part of his estate, and therefore whoever is a beneficiary has a right to the sperm. Yet because parts of the human body are not considered property, it would be difficult to argue that sperm, or in fact any part of a human body, can be inherited along with a house and Canada Savings Bonds.

A further question arises if a widow is impregnated with her late husband's sperm. Does the estate of the late husband have a legal obligation to support the offspring? This is another question that should be considered before such arrangements are made.

A similar question arises if the sperm bank wishes to destroy the late husband's sperm and the widow wishes to prevent this. At issue is who has legal control over the sperm. There would appear to be no legal right on the part of the widow over the sperm unless there is a contract providing for it.

Artificial Insemination by a Donor (AID)

Much artificial insemination uses sperm donated by someone other than the husband, usually because the sperm count of the husband is too low to impregnate the wife. Sometimes the sperm of the husband is mixed with the sperm of the donor, so that there is always the possibility that the offspring may be from the husband, but not necessarily.

Since the impregnation is now not necessarily the result of the union of a husband and a wife, there are legal implications. It was held some years ago that artificial insemination of a wife by someone other than the husband without the consent of the husband may be considered adultery. As highly criticized as that decision has been, it remains a potential legal difficulty. It is therefore extremely important that artificial insemination by a donor, even when the sperm is mixed with that of the husband, be documented as receiving the fully informed consent of the husband.

If the sperm is exclusively that of the donor, it will be clear that the child is not that of the husband but only that of the wife. The question is then whether the husband has any legal responsibility for the child. Should he simply accept the responsibility or should he go through formal proceedings to adopt the child? Adopting the child would certainly make the situation absolutely clear. In any case, legal advice should be obtained before artificial insemination is performed.

Artificial insemination by a donor may create other legal problems. A husband and a wife who resort to artificial insemination by a donor frequently wish to give the impression that the child is their joint offspring. Therefore, they want from the sperm bank some assurance that the child will have at least some of the characteristics of the parents; they probably do not want to have a child whose physical appearance, such as skin colour, is obviously not inherited from either party. The parents may also not want a child who may inherit any genetic diseases from the donor.

The question is whether the parents have a right to these characteristics. Much depends on the contract between the parents and the sperm bank or those who facilitated the donation. It is unlikely that any such contract would make guarantees. However, it could be argued that with respect to genetic diseases, the failure to test for them might be considered negligence and not a failure to warrant that the sperm is safe from disease.

Theoretically, a parent of a child born with a disease may take action against the sperm donor for failing to disclose information that could endanger the child or even the mother. There might also be the possibility of a criminal prosecution. The practical problem is, though, to be able to find the donor (who is usually anonymous) and be able to prove the action of the donor and the link between it and the injury.

In Vitro Fertilization (IVF)

A recent development is that of in vitro fertilization, in which one or more eggs are removed from the mother's ovary. Fertilization takes place outside the body, followed by an incubation period and then transfer of the embryo into the uterus. This overcomes various problems of infertility, such as blocked fallopian tubes. Variants of IVF have been developed, including gamete intrafallopian transfer (GIFT), in which eggs and sperm are transferred unfertilized into a fallopian tube.

As in artificial insemination by a husband, there should be no legal difficulties so long as the sperm is from the husband and the egg is from his wife, and the fertilized egg is to be placed back into his wife. If, however, in vitro fertilization took place using the sperm of a donor or eggs from a donor, legal problems arise. Even though the law assumes that the offspring of a married couple is the legitimate child of that couple, that assumption can be overturned by evidence to the contrary.

Because of the advances of modern technology, many different combinations are now possible. The problems concern the relationship between the mother and her husband, and between the donor of the sperm or the egg, and the child. Do the donors have any liability towards the child? Because the legal implications are uncertain, all parties should seek legal advice and have appropriate documentation prepared regarding their understanding of their various positions and obligations.

Surrogate Motherhood

In surrogate motherhood, the woman who carries the foetus and subsequently bears the child has no intention of keeping the child and being its mother. In some cases the surrogate mother has been artificially inseminated with the sperm of the husband of the woman who intends to be the "mother." In other cases she may carry an embryo resulting from the egg and sperm of another couple, solely to provide a womb. The intention is that on birth the baby will go to the biological parents.

These arrangements, whereby a woman who gives birth to a baby is expected to hand over the baby to someone else who claims "rights" to it, are full of legal difficulties in Canada. Family law in Canada does not depend so much on whether someone has any legal rights to a baby. A court will examine what is in the best interests of the child regardless of what various adults have agreed to. In fact, there is some opinion in Canada that an agreement among the parties involved as to their rights and responsibilities over the child has no legal effect whatsoever. Parties may enter into such an agreement and carry it out without any legal issues being raised. It is when the woman who bears the child objects to giving it up, or the supposed parents refuse to take it, that legal problems arise.

If money is involved in paying a woman for the use of her womb and body, the legal problems may be even more serious. Such an arrangement may not only be unenforceable but may run counter to provincial legislation relating to adoption. Provincial legislation may change from time to time, and from province to province, so there may be difficulties if the parents reside in one province and the baby is to be born in another.

The conclusion, therefore, is that there is much legal uncertainty with respect to surrogate motherhood in Canada, unlike in Great Britain, where by legislation it is prohibited, and in the United States, where it has been dealt with by the courts. Anyone considering these arrangements in Canada should receive extensive legal advice before proceeding, so that they will fully understand the uncertainties and possible legal problems they may face.

Those who become involved in any way in the procreation of children outside the husband-wife setting should fully understand that the birth of a child may have a dramatic effect on the attitudes of all parties. Regardless of all good intentions before any procedures are commenced, the birth of a child may radically alter the positions of the parties, who will then demand rights that were never thought of previously.

The situation to be avoided is the type of lawsuit that has faced American courts, in which there is a conflict between the woman who is giving birth to the baby and the biological parents. The cost and emotional trauma of such a case can be high. So many of the issues have never been dealt with by the courts or governments, and therefore the uncertainty in trying to find solutions through litigation may be a price many may not be willing, or able, to pay.

Summary of Principles

1. There are no legal problems affecting the marital relations of the parties or the relationship between the parents and the child if both the sperm and the egg come from the married couple, regardless of the method of fertilization and impregnation.

2. When either the sperm or any egg is donated, the parents of the offspring have a right to ensure that the collection, handling and use of the sperm and the egg were conducted according to reasonable standards.

3. In many aspects of the storage, handling and testing of human matter for the purposes of procreation, standards have not yet been developed, which makes the rights of the parties unclear and difficult to enforce.

4. Any bank in choosing sperm or other procreative material may not be responsible for the quality of the material unless such issues are previously settled by contract.

5. The question of who will control the frozen sperm in the event of the death of the donor should be settled before the sperm is placed in the sperm bank.

6. Many of the issues arising from surrogate motherhood are not settled in Canadian law and may not be able to be settled by the parties by contract; therefore, the parties should not assume that they have certain rights with respect to the offspring without receiving legal advice before entering an arrangement.

16

CIRCUMCISION

ONE OF THE MOST ANCIENT religious rituals is frequently controversial, that of male circumcision. This procedure involves the surgical removal of the foreskin of the penis. It is a procedure carried out by Jews and Moslems throughout the world.

The procedure is usually performed when the child is young. In the case of Jews it takes place on the eighth day after birth, unless there is a medical reason for a delay. The Jewish ritual may take place at home or in a hospital. No anaesthetic is used, and the person performing the ritual may be a doctor but usually is a non-medical person specially trained to perform ritual circumcision.

The purpose of male circumcision by Jews and Moslems is purely religious, not medical. However, some studies suggest significant medical advantages to the practice. These include lower risks of penile cancer, of cervical cancer in the sexual partners of circumcised males, and of contracting AIDS. It also permits greater cleanliness of the penis, thus lessening the chance of infection. There do not appear to be any medical disadvantages.

Over the years various trends have emerged. At times circumcision has been in vogue, and at other times not. Its popularity has also varied from country to country, with the practice being much more popular in North America than in Europe. Many parents have their sons circumcised for the medical advantages, whereas Jews and Moslems have the ritual performed solely for non-medical reasons.

When adult males are circumcised, it is invariably for medical reasons alone, though it is occasionally done for those who are converting and wish to follow the religious practice.

The Legal Implications of Male Circumcision

The first legal implication arising out of male circumcision is that of consent. (See chapter 4, "Consent to Treatment.") If circumcision is to be performed on an adult for whatever reason, a valid and full consent must be obtained. If the procedure is to be performed for therapeutic reasons, the patient has a right to be informed of the risks both of having it performed and of not having it performed, as well as of the benefits and any reasonable alternatives. This is no different than with any other procedure.

If there are no therapeutic reasons for the procedure, the patient has a right to be told of everything, since there is no reason to withhold any information from him.

The matter of consent with a child is much more complicated. Canadian courts have not yet had to deal with the problem of a child who, on achieving adulthood or through someone acting on his behalf, sued on the basis that the consent of the parents was not valid. (See chapter 7, "Treatment of Children.")

It could be argued that the Supreme Court of Canada case of *Re Eve* could apply to circumcision of children. That case prevented the sterilization of a mentally retarded child on the basis that it was not performed for her benefit even though the mother had consented. Because the medical advantages of a circumcision are present but are only statistical, a court may very well say that the procedure is not for the benefit of the child. The medical advantages may not be considered significant since the procedure is not considered necessary to prevent various problems of the uncircumcised male. The argument would then have to rest on the grounds that since an uncircumcised Jewish child may feel alienated from other Jews, the procedure is for his benefit. This argument would apply to Moslem children as well, but not to non-Jewish, non-Moslem children. The issue of constitutional rights would also be raised.

A further issue is that of the standard that is required in the performance of a circumcision. If a physician performs the operation, the standards to which the patient is entitled are those of the average, reasonable and prudent physician in the circumstances. The 1988 British Columbia Supreme Court case of *Bera v. Marr* concerned a 26-year-old who had been circumcised fourteen years before. The operation caused his penis to deviate to the left, a result, according to the court, of the negligence of the urologist in removing too much skin. The Ontario Supreme Court dealt with a similar accusation, but in that case it was found that the circumcision was done in a normal, competent manner.

The problem arises as to the standards to which the patient has a right if someone who is not a physician does the procedure. Since the person is not a doctor but is doing a procedure that ordinarily a doctor does, are the standards of the medical profession imposed? The patient, or in most cases the parents of the patient, knew that the person was not a doctor. It is difficult to determine what standards must be met, though it may be argued that the patient is entitled to the average, reasonable and prudent standards of anyone doing such a procedure.

A fascinating and largely academic legal argument is whether a person who is not a doctor can legally perform a ritual circumcision, or is such a person practising medicine without a licence? The answer would likely be that this person is not practising medicine but rather carrying out a religious ritual.

Many circumcisions are carried out in hospital by non-physicians. The parents certainly do not have a legal right to have this done, since only members of the medical staff have the privilege of using hospital facilities, equipment and staff. There is also no legal right to have a circumcision performed by a physician who does not wish to do it, just as there is no legal right to have a physician perform any elective procedure.

Female Circumcision

The practice of female circumcision, which is performed in a number of African countries, has been gaining attention in the West. The results of the procedure have been seen among immigrants to Canada, and there is some concern that Canadian physicians may be asked to perform it.

The practice is particularly widespread in Somalia, Ethiopia, Sudan, Egypt and Nigeria. It is not a religious ritual but is purely cultural and is regarded as an initiation rite for girls aged eight to thirteen.

There are various degrees of female circumcision, which may involve both the labia majora and labia minora on each side, as well as the clitoris. The lower part of the vagina may also be scarred. The vulva is then sutered, leaving a small opening for menstrual and urine flow. So far the practice is not specifically prohibited by Canadian law, though physicians may face disciplinary action for performing it. The practice would be regarded as unprofessional conduct involving a non-therapeutic procedure that is extremely harmful and has no medical benefits. It may also be regarded as a crime under the Criminal Code. If a non-physician carries out the procedure in Canada, a similar result is likely.

Unlike male circumcision, female circumcision has no medical advantages, and can have serious long-term disadvantages, including severe urological problems and problems during birth, menstruation and intercourse.

Summary of Principles

1. There is no right to a non-therapeutic male circumcision.
2. A patient may have a right to a therapeutic circumcision if there is a therapeutic reason for performing it, and it is required by average, reasonable and prudent medical standards.
3. A patient having a circumcision has a right to have it performed according to current standards in the same way as any other medical or surgical procedure.

4. A mentally competent male can consent to a circumcision according to the same principles respecting consent to any other procedure.

5. The question of whether the parents of an infant can consent to a non-therapeutic circumcision raises a number of unanswered questions, but as a matter of practice the consent of the parents is accepted.

6. There is no right to have a hospital allow a non-physician to perform a circumcision on its premises.

7. A female patient does not have a right to have a circumcision, and is most likely prohibited from having one in Canada. Nothing prevents a Canadian from having the procedure performed in another country.

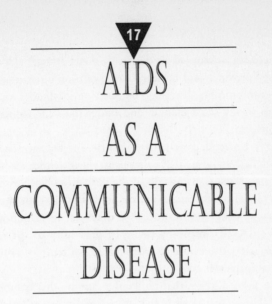

AIDS
AS A
COMMUNICABLE
DISEASE

AIDS in the Social Context

SELDOM HAS A DISEASE attracted so much media attention, so much fear and so much misunderstanding as has AIDS. The chance of dying of AIDS in most Western countries is small compared with the major killers of heart disease, cancer and motor vehicle accidents. This does not mean that AIDS is unimportant or not serious. For a time its rapid rate of increase was frightening. While this rate now seems to be more or less stable in Western countries, this is not the case in many parts of the Third World.

One may argue that there is nothing that distinguishes AIDS from any other communicable disease with which society has been dealing for thousands of years. There have been plenty of other diseases that were life-threatening, had no cure and carried a social stigma. Leprosy and tuberculosis come immediately to mind.

Society has attempted to deal with these through the legal system. Every province and territory has legislation governing the control of communicable diseases. The question is whether AIDS can be dealt with in the same manner and under the same legislation and regulations.

It may be argued that AIDS is different because the human immunodeficiency virus (HIV) that causes it is neither air-borne nor water-borne. Most transmission of the virus takes place through sexual contact, either heterosexual or homosexual. This means that unlike most other communicable diseases, in which a person becomes infected simply by being in proximity to the source of infection, AIDS infection is much more difficult to contract. It requires taking action.

It was argued, then, that unlike the case in other communicable diseases, those infected with AIDS were not "innocent" parties. The use of this word introduced a moral and even theological element into discussions on the subject. This undoubtedly influenced the development of legal responses.

Despite the public controversy and finally the public realization that AIDS was indeed a public health problem and not merely a problem restricted to an unpopular subculture on the fringes of society, the legal responses to AIDS were not innovative.

It was recognized fairly early that before a person develops AIDS they are what is known as HIV-positive, in that they have a virus that invariably goes on to develop into the disease, though this might take many years to come about. During that period they are contagious and can pass on the virus to others.

Communicable Disease Legislation

In the past, society was largely concerned with one issue in the control of communicable diseases, and that was the spread of the disease. As a result, throughout the world communicable disease legislation has been designed to control the spread of disease. Legislation of this type has a long history. The Book of Leviticus, for example, deals extensively with the control of leprosy; when compared with more recent legislation on communicable diseases, the measures are not substantially different.

Because people who are HIV-positive can pass along the virus to others, even though they do not technically have a disease they are in the same state as people who have a communicable disease. HIV-positivity and AIDS were added to the list of communicable diseases of many provinces and territories.

Communicable disease legislation attempts to control the spread of a disease and thus protect the public by doing two things. The first is to isolate the person who has the disease by placing them in quarantine. Patients may under some legislation be quarantined in their residence, where they would not be permitted contact with members of the general public. They may also be quarantined in a public institution. In the past this was the common practice for those who had tuberculosis.

The second step in this process is to force the individual to undergo treatment to remove their danger.

By using these two methods, public health legislation removed two basic legal rights from patients. The first was the right to remain free from imprisonment. Ordinarily, if this right is removed the victim could sue for false imprisonment. The second was the right to be free of bodily interference. Everyone has the legal right to refuse medical treatment regardless of their need for the treatment. Even though the process by which these rights are removed differs from province to province, and country to country, the basic principles behind communicable disease legislation are the same.

Adding AIDS and HIV-positive status to the list of communicable diseases under this legislation caused certain difficulties. AIDS is not like yellow fever or diptheria. A person infected with those diseases can pass along the disease merely by being close to others. Therefore, isolating the person in quarantine would prevent the spread of the disease.

In the case of HIV and AIDS, an infected person cannot pass along the disease by merely being near others. Researchers tell us that a very specific act must take place, usually sexual intercourse or sharing intravenous needles, though it can also be transmitted by blood transfusions, at birth or through needle stick injuries during surgery. The virus must directly enter the bloodstream. Therefore, the method used in communicable disease legislation to control most communicable diseases is not applicable to the control of AIDS. It may be argued, however, that preventing an infected person from mixing with others will also prevent sexual intercourse and the sharing of intravenous needles.

Because it is such a draconian method of control, no country has used quarantine to control AIDS, except Cuba.

The second problem with applying communicable disease legislation to the control of AIDS is that forced treatment is inappropriate. One cannot force an HIV-infected person to take treatment, since at the present time there is no treatment.

An Infected Person's Right to Services

As with leprosy and the bubonic plague in years gone by, AIDS creates a fear among many almost to the point of hysteria. As a result, people who are known or even thought to be infected may be refused a vast array of services and opportunities, from accommodation to employment to insurance to health care. The question is whether it is legal to discriminate against a person who is infected with HIV or AIDS. Most human rights legislation in Canada prohibits discrimination against those who have a physical disability. Being infected is undoubtedly a physical disability.

If the service is not open to the general public it may be possible to discriminate, such as in the case of insurance. Insurance is offered only for those who meet certain physical and health criteria.

The most difficult issue is whether a provider of a health service such as a doctor or a dentist can legally refuse to accept a patient who is HIV-positive. The debate centres on whether a doctor, dentist or other health professional is offering a public service and, therefore, is subject to anti-discrimination legislation. By and large, the attitude of human rights commissions is that health professionals cannot discriminate on the basis of infection. Any current patient cannot be dropped on becoming HIV-positive.

The only way a health professional may be able to discriminate would be on the basis of not having either the expertise or the facilities to handle a person who is infected. Considering the simplicity of the minimal precautions that are necessary — precautions that should be followed with *any* patient — this would be very difficult to argue. The same would be true with hospitals, long-term-care facilities, clinics and home care agencies. Some health care agencies may be able to refuse an AIDS patient not because the patient has a disease but because they do not have the staff trained to provide the necessary care.

Persons who are infected also have a right in many provinces to be protected against discrimination in employment. However, if a person cannot physically perform the particular job, this is a valid basis for denying employment or dismissing the person from employment. As well, if it can be shown that the infected person may pass on the disease as part of the employment, employment could be denied or terminated. However, given the increased knowledge about the difficulty of infecting others, it would be very difficult to prove this.

The infected person not only has rights to not be denied employment and to not be terminated except according to the usual legal requirements, but also has the right to not be harassed while an employee. The harassment may force the employee to resign. The law would regard this as a constructive dismissal and treat it as if the person had been improperly fired.

The Right to Confidentiality

Most people do not want the world knowing about their illnesses. In some cases, strenuous efforts are made to keep it quiet, such as when a political leader has a terminal illness. However, because of the social stigma associated with AIDS, many who are infected are anxious to keep this information under wraps. Gradually, as AIDS has become more common and a large number of people who are well known die of it, it is becoming more socially acceptable, but it is still not the same as having a hip replacement.

The law relating to confidentiality in health matters generally applies to AIDS and HIV status. (See chapter 9, "Patient Records, Access and Confidentiality.") Those who are infected have the right, however uncertain it is, to have that information kept confidential unless they consent to its release. In some cases there is legislation to establish this right. In other cases, it is based on what lawyers think the courts might do if someone sued for breach of confidentiality.

People usually do not sue, because of the cost, because the information would get wider publicity and because it would be difficult to show that any injury had occurred. If a health professional released the information, disciplinary action may be taken on the basis of breach of professional ethics.

Despite this right, the law is full of loopholes, and the realities of the situation are that the right is very watered down. Communicable disease legislation usually requires that cases be reported to public health officials. Because many people who might be HIV-positive may therefore be afraid to be tested, some provinces have allowed anonymous testing.

Legislation frequently prevents the breach of confidentiality in hospitals and in the medicare system. However, this is often where practicality intervenes. What is meant by confidentiality? On entering a hospital, or any health institution, an infected person is to be treated by a large number of people directly and indirectly. Because of the danger of infection and because of the need to care for a patient in an appropriate manner, information about the patient's illness must be communicated to a great number of staff. Because of the availability of the patient's records to staff who may have no involvement with the patient, any semblance of true confidentiality does not and cannot exist. Unless the staff is extremely well disciplined, comments made in corridors and in the cafeteria are inevitable.

A further exception to any right to confidentiality is that of a warning to family, partner, friends, schools and employers. It appears that there is a duty on doctors and perhaps others who have information about their patients that might harm third parties to warn those third parties. Because of the nature of AIDS, an infected person can cause no harm to fellow students or co-workers. Therefore, there is no duty to inform them of the patient's condition. Similarly, there is no duty to inform family members except a spouse who, one can assume, will have intercourse with the patient and, therefore, be at some risk of becoming infected.

A Toronto doctor was disciplined for not informing the wife of an infected patient because he assumed that they no longer had sex. The wife had a right to be told.

Based on these principles, it would appear that the lover of a patient also has a legal right to know of the patient's condition, and thus the patient has no right to have this information kept secret from the lover. It is highly questionable that the duty to tell is fulfilled if the patient assures the doctor that the lover will be informed by the patient.

On death, it can also be argued that a hospital or nursing home has a legal duty to inform the funeral home that the patient died of AIDS or complications arising from AIDS. Even if the family objects to this information being divulged, the risk of embalmers becoming infected despite all precautions may be significant. They therefore have a right to this information, so that special care can be taken, or so that they can refuse to embalm the remains.

HIV Testing

One of the most controversial AIDS issues is the HIV test, the blood test that determines whether a person has been infected with the virus that causes AIDS.

The issue arises largely in hospitals, where a battery of blood and other tests are taken and an HIV test may be included. It is often argued by health professionals that once a patient consents to blood tests, the hospital and its staff have the authority to conduct whatever tests they wish on the blood taken.

The problem is that there are significant non-medical risks in knowing that one is infected. It means having to answer yes to the question "Are you HIV positive?" It may result in discrimination in many areas of life regardless of whether that discrimination is illegal.

While there is no definite legal position on the matter, it would appear that there is a right to refuse HIV testing, and therefore the test should not be performed without the consent of the patient. Before consent can be validly given, the patient has a right to know the nature and purpose of the test, the risks and benefits and any alternatives. The patient must also be told the risks and benefits of not having the test. Finally, the patient must be given the opportunity to ask questions. As with all matters of consent, the patient must be mentally capable of consenting and have the legal capacity to do so.

There is a question whether a hospital can require HIV testing before surgery so that staff can take special precautions so as not to become infected, particularly by needle-stick injuries. This question has never been fully answered. It is highly doubtful that a patient could be refused surgery for failing to consent to a test that has nothing to do with the surgical procedure.

If, however, a needle-stick injury occurs, a related question arises. Can the patient be tested to determine whether the staff member has been exposed as a result of the injury? In this case there is a very good argument to support testing even against the consent of the patient.

Because of the consequences of being tested positive, the patient has a right to a repeat test because of the risk of a "false positive," in which the laboratory result was incorrect. One problem is that of the false negative in which a patient continues to act as if there was no infection. The question then arises whether the lover of the person tested can seek compensation for becoming infected as a result of negligent testing. They cannot if there was no negligence in the conduct of the test.

The Right to Be Free from AIDS

Patients in hospitals may be exposed to AIDS primarily through two means, tainted blood transfusions and organ transplants. In both cases, tests are now conducted, though in the case of transfusions, many Canadians contracted the disease before tests were either available or conducted. As a result, numerous lawsuits are pending across the country brought by patients who required blood transfusions. Since blood screening was made more rigorous, the risk of receiving tainted blood is significantly lower.

In any situation in which there is a risk of being infected, the patient has a right to be told. However, even if the patient is not told, it might be very difficult to win a lawsuit unless there was negligence. It would be difficult to show that consent would have been refused by a reasonable person who knew about the risk.

A controversial issue is whether a patient has a right to be informed that the doctor or dentist providing service is HIV-positive. Both the Canadian Medical Association and the Canadian Dental

Association have taken the position that it is not necessary for their members who are infected to advise their patients of this fact. The rationale behind this position is that the risk of a health professional passing along the disease to a patient is very small, especially if proper precautions are taken.

The issue, however, is not whether the risk is large or small. The issue is whether it is the patient or the doctor or dentist who should decide whether the risk to the patient should be accepted. The patronizing attitude that "the doctor knows best" is a thing of the past. It is the patient who decides what if any risks shall be taken. Even if those risks are small, it is the patient who must make the decision whether those risks to his or her body will be taken. To do this, the patient has a right to know whether any health professional providing a service that could pose a risk is HIV-positive.

Travel

Many countries have become concerned about "importing" AIDS and have imposed requirements that visitors have a certificate stating that they are HIV-negative before being granted an entry visa. Sometimes this requirement applies only to student or work visas, or visas for a particular length of stay.

As a matter of practice, it does not apply to countries to which Canadian nationals do not need a visa. It may be argued that this offers little protection, since anyone with an HIV-free certificate is only free of infection on the date that the certificate is issued, and in fact may be HIV-positive by the time they visit another country. None the less, those who are positive have no right to an entry visa, since a visa to a foreign country is never obtained as a right in any case.

To determine the requirements of a country to which a visit is contemplated, travellers should contact the embassy or consulate of that country. Travellers should not rely on information obtained through a travel agency, which may be out of date or inaccurate.

Summary of Principles

1. Persons infected with HIV or AIDS may in theory be subject to confinement under public health quarantine legislation, but in fact this legislation is not used.

2. Persons who test HIV-positive may be reported to public health officials.

3. As a general rule, discrimination in employment, accommodation and public services may not be denied under most human rights legislation.

4. Patients who are infected with HIV or AIDS have a right to have this fact kept confidential by health care providers except where legislation requires it to be reported and except where there is a duty to notify persons who could be infected, including other health personnel caring for the infected person and those who would ordinarily be having sexual relations with the infected person.

5. Patients who are to receive blood transfusions and organ transplants have a legal right to be informed of the risk, however small, of being infected with HIV, as part of their right to give an informed consent.

6. Patients have a right to be informed that the doctor or dentist or other personnel treating them is infected with HIV, regardless of how small the risk of infection may be.

7. Infected persons may be barred from a number of countries on the basis of their infection.

MENTAL
ILLNESS

18

MENTAL ILLNESS HAS HAD a long and shameful legal history. Right into living memory, Canadian society and its laws continued to refer to "lunatic asylums" and "asylums for the harmless insane." Even today, the mentally ill are regarded with suspicion and not treated in the same way as those who are physically ill. Mental illness is one of the few forms of illness that continues to be dealt with in separate legislation. (At one time in Canada numerous acts dealt with specific diseases, including tuberculosis, venereal disease and leprosy.) Most jurisdictions have a mental health act, though there are exceptions, such as Nova Scotia, where legislation dealing with mental illness is part of the hospitals legislation.

Canada also continues to have specialized hospitals for the treatment of mental illness. However, most patients suffering from mental illness are treated either by their family physicians, by psychiatrists on referral from a family physician, in a mental health centre or other out-patient clinic, or in the psychiatric department of a general hospital. By and large, mental health legislation deals only with patients in specialized mental institutions or psychiatric hospitals. Despite the trend to treat mental illness on an out-patient basis, or at least in general hospitals, the legislation still concentrates on patients who are in psychiatric hospitals.

It should be noted that mental health acts have little or nothing to do with mental health. They specifically concentrate on mental illness and then only the more severe forms of mental illness.

At one time it was assumed that a person who was believed to be mentally ill was totally incompetent, dangerous and perhaps possessed. It is only within the past twenty or thirty years that a more liberal attitude has been taken towards mental illness, and the legislation has followed suit. However, it has by and large been a liberalization of the old form of legislation.

All patients, whether they are mentally or physically ill, enjoy the basic civil rights of any member of society. That a person is mentally ill does not by itself automatically remove legal rights.

The first basic right that remains the same as that of any patient is that when being treated for mental illness, a patient has the right to be treated according to average, reasonable and prudent standards in the circumstances. Because the treatment of mental illness depends so much on the individual patient and the circumstances and is so much a matter of judgement, it is difficult to prove negligence in the care and treatment of the mentally ill. However, there has been a history of lawsuits in Canada in which the families of patients have sued psychiatrists for malpractice when a patient has committed suicide.

The Supreme Court of British Columbia, in the 1992 case of *Stewart v. Noone*, was faced with the question of whether a number of hospital psychiatrists were negligent when a patient attempted suicide and was seriously injured. He had previously attempted suicide and had been diagnosed as manic-depressive. However, just before the attempted suicide in question he was examined by the psychiatrists in hospital, who found no evidence of psychosis, depression or hypomania. As a result he was discharged. Even though the patient became suicidal, the court found that the psychiatrists had applied their psychiatric training in a reasonable manner in finding that *at that time* the patient was not suicidal. That the patient was later suicidal did not mean that the psychiatrists were negligent. They had met the legally required standard in caring for him and in making their diagnosis.

The second basic and unchanged right that the mentally ill patient has is the right to refuse treatment regardless of the need for the treatment. Even if a patient is suffering from delusions, the rejection of treatment may be valid if the patient is mentally capable of making the decision. As long as the patient has the mental capability to understand the information the law says must be given in order to make a valid decision, the consent or the refusal to consent is valid. That the person is suffering from mental illness does not by itself make the decision invalid. (See chapter 4, "Consent to Treatment.")

The Effect of Legislation

Every province has attempted to remove or at least modify these basic rights of persons who are mentally ill. At one time, a person who was considered to be suffering from what was called a mental disorder could be "committed" to a "mental hospital" by a doctor. This had two effects. The first was that the patient could be forcibly taken to a psychiatric hospital and confined. The second was that the person, once in the mental hospital, could be treated for that mental illness against his or her will. Even though the person may have been mentally capable of refusing hospitalization and treatment, the right to do so had been lost.

The social attitude towards mental illness has changed in the past half-century. It was recognized that society could accept in its midst many mentally ill people who were not a risk to other people or to themselves. Legislation therefore changed and generally became confined to those who were suffering from a mental disorder and were a danger either to themselves or to others. The criteria by which a person can be confined to a psychiatric facility differ slightly from province to province. How a person can be forcibly sent to and detained in a facility also differs somewhat across the country. Legislation designates who can initiate action that results in a person being confined to a psychiatric facility, including a physician, a court, the police, or family, friends or neighbours.

In addition, there are differences in what happens once a person is detained, such as whether the law simply authorizes detention or also permits involuntary treatment. The legislation also specifies where the person can be detained. This may be restricted to psychiatric hospitals or may include other places if there is no hospital, such as a jail, at least temporarily. This may include designated areas of general hospitals.

The length of time the person can be held is limited, and this also differs across the country, as does the procedure necessary to either release the person or to allow him or her to remain as a voluntary patient.

Most provinces have a system whereby the patient can appeal the various decisions that are made about involuntary detention or treatment. Appeal boards are set up differently across Canada, and the procedures used to appeal and the various rights that are given to patients before these boards also differ. All procedures however, must meet the basic standards set out in the Canadian Charter of Rights and Freedoms.

Because of the abuses of the past, many provinces have specifically given to patients in psychiatric facilities, whether they are involuntary or not, numerous other rights, such as the right to consult a lawyer, the right to receive and send letters and the right to make and receive telephone calls. The right of access to hospital records is frequently dealt with in legislation. (See chapter 9, "Patient Records, Access and Confidentiality.")

Concerns about certain types of psychiatric treatment have prompted some provinces to control the use of these treatments. Some legislation controls and restricts the use of psychosurgery such as lobotomies. Others control the use of electro-convulsive therapy.

Because all of these patients' rights or restrictions on rights arise from provincial legislation, there is no uniformity across the country. Patients who are concerned about their rights should therefore consult the mental health legislation of their province or territory.

Modern mental health legislation has not only made it more difficult to have patients' rights removed, it has also made it more difficult to have patients receive the care they require. Unless a patient's condition specifically fits the criteria for committal and detention, an unwilling patient may go without care. Social workers and police frequently see the mentally ill wandering about the streets or living in squalor. As long as they are not a danger to themselves or others (or whatever the provincial criteria are), nothing can be done for them.

The Criminal Code and the Mentally Ill

A particular problem arises when a person who is charged with a criminal offence is found to be mentally ill. The situation is dealt with extensively in the Criminal Code of Canada, but it becomes a problem when the person is sent to a hospital. The question then arises as to whether the person falls within the federal law under the Criminal Code or provincial mental health legislation, and whether the two bodies of law conflict.

A person who is charged with a criminal offence can be found unfit to stand trial because he or she is not mentally capable of instructing legal counsel and, in fact, may not understand what is occurring. Even if a person is fit to stand trial but is found to have been mentally incapable of being held responsible for the crime, that person cannot be punished. Section 672 of the Criminal Code sets out the rights of such a person extensively, since that person can be sent to a psychiatric institution for treatment. There is also a review board under the Criminal Code to which the person can appeal. Because of the intricacies of the system, it is important that anyone finding themselves in this situation obtain detailed legal advice regarding their rights under the Code.

What Can a Mental Patient Do and Not Do?

A person who is suffering from a mental illness is not necessarily incompetent, just as a person who is mentally retarded is not necessarily incompetent. The question that must always be asked is: Is the person incompetent, or more accurately incapable of doing something? Every province and territory has legislation that allows a court to declare a person incompetent — that is, incapable of handling his or her own affairs. A guardian is appointed on the person's behalf and the person is no longer allowed to perform various acts.

Provinces also have public trustees or public guardians to look after the property of persons who are not capable of looking after it themselves and who do not have private guardians. Some patients in psychiatric facilities have such arrangements made.

It is possible for a person who is mentally ill to perform many legal acts but not others. The question that must be asked in each and every case is whether the person is mentally capable of understanding the criteria necessary for the performance of that act. A person may not be mentally capable of writing a will, because he lacks what is called testamentary capacity and does not understand that he is signing a document that will distribute his property after he dies. Yet the same person may be able to vote, since some would say the mental capacity required is not as great.

Because of mental incapacity, regardless of whether the person is a patient or suffering from illness or not, a person may not be held responsible for a civil wrong, such as assault or negligence, or responsible for a criminal offence or an offence under another law. Such a person, though, may enter into marriage or enter into a contract.

It is possible that if a mentally ill person is responsible for acts such as assault, battery or negligence, someone else can be held liable for that person. If a mentally ill person, for example, has a propensity to strike out at others and is a resident of a long-term-care facility, the facility, knowing that there is a reasonable foreseeability of the patient doing harm, is under a duty to take reasonable precautions to prevent such harm.

If the patient does strike out and assault someone, the victim may sue the facility for negligence in failing to take reasonable steps to prevent that action.

Each of these acts, negligence, entering into a contract, or a criminal office, must be assessed on its own merits on the basis of the mental capacity of the individual at the time. It is possible for a person to be mentally capable of performing a particular act or being held responsible for a particular act on one day but not the next, because of a change in mental condition. Legal advice should be obtained in each case.

Summary of Principles

1. A psychiatric patient has the same legal rights and responsibilities as any other person unless those rights or responsibilities are specifically removed by legislation.

2. Provincial mental health legislation provides a procedure by which a person can be involuntarily confined and frequently treated in a psychiatric facility without consent, but for such confinement and treatment the legislation must be strictly adhered to.

3. A person who is mentally ill may not be able to stand trial or be held criminally responsible for a criminal act, in which case the Criminal Code allows for confinement in a psychiatric facility, with various appeal mechanisms.

4. That a person is mentally ill does not by itself mean that a person cannot perform certain legal acts or be held responsible for them, since much depends on whether the person had the mental capacity to be responsible for that particular act.

5. A psychiatric patient has the same right as any other patient to receive services according to average, reasonable and prudent standards.

19

RESEARCH

ON

PATIENTS

ADVANCES IN MEDICAL SCIENCE depend on research. At some point, research must go beyond the laboratory into the hospitals and even into doctors' offices. The result is that new techniques, new drugs and new treatments at some point are tried on patients. This is the only way that medical science can advance. The issue is, where does this leave the patient and what are the patient's rights?

Research can be the use of new products, techniques or drugs with an attempt being made to care for or treat the patient. It can also be the use of a procedure or the collection of data on someone with a particular condition to learn more about that condition, but with no attempt being made to treat the patient.

The legal principles involved are essentially the same in both cases. They are those that apply to all procedures relating to consent to treatment (see chapter 4, "Consent to Treatment") and negligence (see chapter 5, "Negligence and Standards of Care").

Consent to Research

The basic principle in consent to treatment is that the patient has a right to refuse all or any treatment regardless of whether it is needed. A second principle is that in order to make that decision, the patient has the right to be informed of all material risks — that is, risks that are unusual or significant. The patient has the right to be informed of the benefits and all reasonable alternatives. The same principles apply when research is to be conducted.

If the research involves something new or experimental, in that it has not been completely accepted as a usual form of care, the patient has the legal right to be informed of all potential risks. In some cases, the treatment is not being used for the benefit of the patient at all. It is being used solely to gain scientific knowledge. In such a case, the "patient," who may be perfectly healthy, has the right to be informed of every conceivable risk, since the patient receives no benefit. The doctor cannot withhold information on the basis that it must be balanced with the patient's needs.

If the procedure or treatment is experimental *and* it is hoped that the patient will benefit, full information must also be provided. This information must be balanced with information about the potential benefits. Information must be given that will allow the patient to compare the experimental treatment with the standard usual treatment.

There are no definite guidelines for doctors, except that as treatment moves away from the standard treatment, more and more information must be given to the patient. Of particular importance is that the patient should be told that the treatment is new or experimental. If it is being used for research purposes, the patient should know this and know why the research is being conducted, under whose auspices and what use is to be made of the information.

The research aspect of the case raises the question of confidentiality. (See chapter 9, "Patient Records, Access and Confidentiality.") The patient has a right to ask and to be informed whether personal information will be divulged and to whom. The patient should be informed whether other researchers will be advised and whether they will become involved directly with the patient.

This is particularly important, since the researchers may in fact become involved in the case of the patient even though that is not their primary interest. The difficulty is that the research aspect of the treatment may come into conflict with the treatment aspect, so that the need to obtain information may overcome the need to care for the patient.

Standard of Care

The courts have made it clear that when treatment is being given that is new or experimental, it is not enough to abide by average, reasonable and prudent standards of care. A higher standard of care is required. The purpose of meeting a legally required standard of care is to avoid reasonably foreseeable injury. When experimenting with a new procedure, it is not always possible to know what injuries are reasonably foreseeable. In other cases, the risk of injury may be increased. As a result, the standard of care must be higher.

In an attempt to protect patients, the Medical Research Council of Canada has issued guidelines for the conduct of medical research in Canada. They require that a number of questions be asked before research on humans takes place. Is the research scientifically valid and what are its potential benefits? Should the research take place at the present time? Is the group of research subjects appropriate? What are the risks that can be identified, and which are potential? Is the research ethically acceptable? The guidelines also require the establishment of research ethics boards to review many of these issues. Hospitals also have ethics committees. In addition, the guidelines require that as part of the consent process a rather lengthy list of matters must be made known to the patient, including the reasons for the study, the research techniques and the reason that the patient is being asked to participate.

A Right to Something New

Many patients who have been subjected to the standard form of treatment without success want to try techniques, treatments or drugs that are not fully accepted. Drugs that have not been approved by the federal government may be used through special arrangements. Other techniques may be used, though physicians frequently will refer the matter to their colleagues or an ethics committee because of the uncertainties.

A patient does not have a legal right to have a treatment, a technique, a procedure or a drug that is new or experimental, for which the results are uncertain and which does not fall within the standard practice. This does not mean that it cannot be given, but there is no right to it.

Physicians may in many cases be justified in refusing to try something new or experimental, or even to include a patient in a research project that may have beneficial results. The physician may not have the expertise to administer the care. The hospital may not have the necessary support services. A new drug may be used only at an institution that has a fully approved research program for that drug. The only hope that a patient wanting to go beyond the usual practice has is to seek a referral to someone or some place where experimental drugs or procedures are used.

These guidelines are not law. There is no requirement that they be met, and patients undergoing research do not have a right to have the guidelines followed. In any case, they would not apply to experimental techniques that are not being used as part of a research project.

Summary of Principles

1. Subjects of research, whether it is for their benefit or not, must give a fully informed consent.
2. All the principles of consent for standard care and treatment, including those of legal capacity and mental capability, apply to research.
3. The exception is that the patient of a research method has the right to be informed to a much greater extent than a patient who is subject to ordinary procedures.
4. The patient who is the subject of a research, experiment or new procedure has the right to a higher standard of care than would be required if the procedure were the standard procedure ordinarily used.
5. The patient who is the subject of research project has the right to know who will be given information about the patient's condition.

PART
THREE

20

WHAT

IS THE

LAW?

NEVER BEFORE IN THE HISTORY of this country has "the law" received so much publicity. Television seems to burst with courtroom dramas, mainly from the United States. Trials are covered by the press in the most lurid detail. Medico-legal issues are certain to get the attention of the press, even if the issues are highly speculative. Professors who in the past were kept well closeted in the stuffy halls of academia have become television celebrities, commenting on everything from the right of lesbians to be artificially impregnated to the duty of HIV-positive doctors to inform their patients. Constitutional debates since the 1960s have received so much constant publicity that the attention of the Canadian public has become almost obsessed with the law. Added to this was Canada's tendency to ride on the coat-tails of the United States, picking up on its concentration on consumer advocacy and demanding one's rights. Governments began putting out booklets for the general public telling them what the law is. Canadian publishing saw a virtual explosion of law texts and legal books for the general public. A large selection of American law books are carried in Canadian bookstores, even though the laws do not apply in this country.

Until this growth in the popularity of law, Canadians were satisfied to leave the law to its black-robed practitioners in the hushed and hallowed halls of the courts. For most people, law was divorced from life, except in Agatha Christie dramas and Hollywood films. It spoke a language most people could not understand. (Law schools usually required applicants to have studied Latin, as did medical schools.)

The reality is that "the law" is not what is found in government publications or in "office consolidations" of acts and regulations. This is not to say that this information is incorrect. The problem is that it is taken to be *the* law on the subject, so that when one reads, say, the provincial hospitals act, one assumes one has in one little booklet the law on the subject. This is not true.

These publications can be very useful guides to the law and a reflection of what some of the law is, but they cannot be taken as the entire law on the subject.

Defining the Law

The law can be defined as the study of the relations between people. This relationship is determined in terms of the rights and duties between those people as recognized by the courts. It deals with the relationship between individuals, between individuals and corporations, between individuals or corporations and governments, and between governments. A lawsuit is essentially nothing more than a result of the breakdown of this relationship. The person suing — that is, the plaintiff — is saying that the the person being sued — the defendant — had not fulfilled a legally required duty to the plaintiff, who had a right to whatever it was that the defendant supposedly had a duty to do. The plaintiff, therefore, wants to be compensated by the defendant.

In the realm of patients' rights, the law governs the relationship between, for example, a patient and a physician, a patient and a nurse or a patient and a long-term-care facility. These relationships are expressed in terms of the right of the patient to certain things that the doctor has a duty to do, such as to provide services according to an average, reasonable and prudent standard. The patient also may have certain legal duties towards the doctor, and the doctor certain rights. These rights and duties arise when the relationship has been created — that is, when the health care professional or institution takes on the care of the patient.

Clearly, defining law in this way is not that different than in many other disciplines, such as psychology, sociology, economics and political science, all of which deal with relationships among people. The difference is that the relationships in law are made up of rights and duties flowing between the two parties.

Five premises are found in this definition of law. The first is that law is a reflection of the relationships that *actually* exist between people in society, not the relationships that *should* exist. Law does not tell us how we *should* relate towards one another; that falls within the bounds of morality, ethics and justice. The law reflects the way people *do relate* in society and then imposes that standard on everyone.

The Bible may tell us to love one another; the law does not. Higher social values suggest that we act in a way that is courteous, kind and thoughtful; the law does not. The law therefore reflects the common denominator of social interaction, anything below which society will not tolerate.

There is no doubt that professional ethics play a role in the law, but only because they are accepted as a reflection of those standards that society has accepted. The ultimate goal is that gradually society will accept as common practice the higher moral standards that are now only standards towards which society should strive. Therefore, the study of law is not the study of ethics, even though they deal with the same subjects and often reach the same conclusions.

The second premise of the definition is that because law is a reflection of society, it follows society. It does not lead. When relationships in society change, the law will eventually change to reflect those social changes. The law is slow to change, however. It takes time for courts and governments to become aware of the social changes and to agree that these changes are truly the reality of society, rather than a passing trend or a change among a minority of people. When law tries to lead society, invariably it fails, because society is not truly supportive of the change and will not follow it. It therefore becomes very difficult to enforce social change that is legislated from the top.

Therefore, when lawyers say that a particular law is bad law, they do not mean that it is immoral or unethical. They may mean that it does not clearly or accurately reflect the social reality and is out of step with the way their clients are actually conducting their lives. The law may be out of date or too far ahead of society. It may also be bad law because it conflicts with other legal principles and consequently may cause more disputes than it prevents. It may be bad law because it is unclear and becomes a source of uncertainty and confusion.

The third premise of the definition of law is that, like society, law has many unanswered questions and uncertainties. If the problem in any legal issue is essentially that of morality, ethics or politics, the law may have no answers. Lawyers and law professors can speculate endlessly on what the courts may do if faced with the issue. However, these issues often do not go to court because few people have the temperament, patience or funds to sue in order to decide a highly speculative issue. The law, therefore, cannot solve or even provide direction on all issues affecting patient care under all conceivable circumstances. It can only point to various principles and speculate on how those principles might be applied to the facts and circumstances presented to the court.

The fourth premise is that law does not have a definite rule to suit all situations. Much depends on the circumstances and facts unique to each situation to determine which legal principle should apply and which will not.

The final premise is that since law reflects society, it reflects the society in which it exists. As time passes, society changes, as do social relations. The law responds. Legal principles are applied differently, and sometimes even new principles are developed out of the old.

This is not only a reflection of a society that changes over time. It is also a reflection of the society in a geographic or political jurisdiction. One cannot assume that the law of New York State is the same as that of British Columbia. There may be a great deal of similarity, since the legal systems of those places were brought with settlers from essentially the same place, namely England. Therefore, many legal answers are the same, whether they are found in Manitoba, Prince Edward Island, Pennsylvania or England. Canadian law is becoming increasingly influenced by American legal developments and less so by British developments. This is particularly true in health law, because the health care systems of the United States and Canada, and the way medicine is practised, are so similar.

However, American and Canadian attitudes about many things are different, even though sometimes these differences are subtle. Canadians frequently fail to recognize this. They often assume that American legal problems are also Canadian problems, and therefore American solutions can be applied to Canada. At the same time, when it is convenient, Canadians reject American developments as being totally irrelevant to Canada. This is also not true. Each situation must be judged on its own merits. In many cases certain health law problems have been dealt with in American law and a solution has been found, where in Canada the law has not dealt with the problem. This does not mean that Canadian law would adopt the American solution. The answer may be entirely speculative, and sometimes must remain so. Legal advice may be that in some situations Canadian courts would take the same position as the American courts, whereas in other situations they would not. From a patient's point of view, there will continue to be similarities and differences between the two countries.

What Is the Law and Where Is It From?

The law dealing with any particular issue comes from a number of sources. The major source of law in Canada (except in Quebec) is the common law that is the law as derived from England. In Quebec the basic principles are set out in the Civil Code, which derives from the Napoleonic Code of France.

English common law is really nothing more than tradition. When disputes were taken before the courts in England, the lawyers on each side would ask the courts to come to a decision similar to that decided in previous similar court disputes. In examining previous cases, lawyers and the courts try to derive principles of law that were established in those cases and that could be applied in future cases.

There is no mystery in this process. In everyday life when a decision has to be made in any organization, or any work place, one invariably asks, "What did we do about this last month, or last year?" It does not mean that a similar decision will be made, but there is a feeling that there should be consistency in the decisions so that people affected by them know what to expect.

When English colonies were established, the colonial courts looked to English cases for guidance. To provide a certain measure of consistency throughout the Empire, it was possible to appeal from the colonial courts to what is called the Judicial Committee of the Privy Council, in London. Because this body was bound to follow the principles established by the House of Lords, which was the final court of appeal in Britain, the colonies tended to be very similar in their approach to decision making. Appeals to the Privy Council from Canada were not abolished until 1949, when the Supreme Court of Canada became the final court of appeal here.

A simple example of a principle being applied to a modern situation is that of a battery. The courts long ago decided that every person had a legal right to not be touched by others without consent. Any person who touched another in anger, according to the 1704 case of *Cole v. Turner*, was a battery for which the victim could be compensated even if there was no injury. One can imagine such cases arising out of a donnybrook behind a pub, but the principle can also be applied to a lawsuit brought on the basis of unconsented-to surgery.

Under the English common law system as it is used in Canada, all courts are bound to follow principles of law handed down by higher courts, so that all Canadian courts are bound by the decisions of the Supreme Court of Canada. It is questionable whether Quebec courts are bound by the Supreme Court of Canada if the decision is solely based on principles of English law, which are not applicable under the Quebec legal system.

One provincial court is not bound by a court in another province, however. It is theoretically possible for a decision regarding the rights of a patient handed down by the Court of Appeal in Alberta to be different from that decided by the Court of Appeal in Ontario or New Brunswick. Such a difference, however, is infrequent, because in fact, courts do follow each other.

Similarly, it is possible for one common law country to look at the decisions of courts in other common law countries. Canadian courts do on occasion borrow law from American courts and British courts if there is no judicial experience with that issue at home. Canadian courts adopted, for example, the principle established in New Zealand that a patient has a right to receive answers to questions posed before giving consent to treatment. The House of Lords frequently surveys decisions of other courts in the English-speaking world.

As the years pass, however, the various English common law jurisdictions develop their own societies with their own attitudes, problems and disputes. The law as developed in the courts of those places reflects the uniqueness of those places. As a result, the law of consent where it relates to what a physician must tell a patient is different in Britain than it is in Canada or the United States, where the system is usually referred to as the Anglo-American legal system. The Canadian position is similar to the American position but not completely.

For these reasons, it is important not to assume that reports of decisions in other English common law countries necessarily apply in Canada. It is particularly important not to react to press reports from the United States, which tend to be widely publicized in Canada, without seeking legal advice to determine if in fact a decision is applicable to the rights of patients in Canada.

Quebec, as mentioned, operates under the French civil law system. The principles under that system are derived from the Civil Code, which is interpreted not only by the courts but also by legal authors and commentators. It has its origins in the Napoleonic Code of France and shares traditions with many civil law jurisdictions throughout the world, including the state of Louisiana, Puerto Rico and many former colonies of France. Because Quebec is part of a largely English country, though, some areas of Quebec law are based on English common law. Patients' rights are generally not, though English cases are cited in Quebec courts as additional arguments.

In addition to common law and the Civil Code, law in Canada is derived from statutes — that is, acts of provincial and federal legislatures — along with regulations made by governments as authorized by those acts. Most of these acts are made by provincial legislatures, since under the Canadian Constitution health is a provincial matter. These include hospital acts, acts dealing with nursing homes, mental health legislation and public health acts. It also includes health provisions found in acts dealing with broader subjects, such as schools, penitentiaries, immigration and the provision of services to native peoples.

Acts may give patients rights in addition to those they possess under common law or the Civil Code. They may alter existing rights. They may remove rights, and they may clarify rights that are not clear.

Law is also derived from municipal by-laws and ordinances. These enactments deal largely with public health matters.

One source of law that is often forgotten is hospital by-laws. These can have a profound effect on patients' rights, especially where they relate to the responsibilities of the medical staff. This "legislation" is usually subject to provincial government approval and has the force of law. It cannot conflict with provincial or federal legislation.

Until 1982, this would have been the end of the discussion of the sources of Canadian law as far as parents' rights were concerned. In that year, Canada's constitution, the British North America Act, was gussied up with a new title, the Constitution Act, and with the addition of the Canadian Charter of Rights and Freedoms. Federal and provincial governments could no longer pass legislation that infringed the Charter. Acts dealing with patients' rights were now subject to the scrutiny of the courts, which would determine whether an act or regulation was even valid.

Some of the Charter rights that can conceivably affect patients' rights are found in section 7, which gives to everyone the right to life, liberty and security of the person and the right to not be deprived of these except in accordance with the principles of fundamental justice. It was under this section that the Supreme Court of Canada, in *R. v. Morgentaler et al.* in 1988, struck down section 287 of the Criminal Code, which required all abortions in Canada to be approved by a hospital therapeutic abortion committee, even though that section had been passed by an elected Parliament.

Section 9, giving everyone the right to not be arbitrarily detained or imprisoned, may also affect patients' rights, particularly under psychiatric legislation or quarantine provisions of communicable disease legislation. (See chapter 18, "Mental Illness.")

Summary of Principles

1. Law is the study of the relations between people as expressed in terms of the recognized legal rights and duties each has towards the other.

2. A lawsuit results from the breakdown of that relationship.

3. Law reflects the way people in society actually treat each other at a standard beneath which society will not tolerate, and not the ethical standards that society would like to see people achieve.

4. The law that establishes the rights and duties is derived from principles taken from past court decisions (or, in Quebec, from the Civil Code), provincial and federal statutes and regulations, municipal by-laws and ordinances, hospital by-laws and the Canadian Charter of Rights and Freedoms.

5. Canadian law and American law derived from the same English sources but have developed differently as their societies have developed apart from that of Britain.

21

TO WHOM

DO YOU

COMPLAIN

AND HOW?

A POPULAR WORD IN OUR PUBLIC LIFE seems to be *advocacy.* In every aspect of our dealings with others, we are constantly told to be advocates. Stand up for our rights. Speak up. Thousands are taking this advice, and as a result professional discipline bodies across Canada are swamped with complaints. The courts are busier than ever, and the law schools are cranking out lawyers all ready to fight, argue and spat. Whether advocacy improves health care is questionable. Unfortunately, complaints arise only after it is too late.

A consumer requiring a service seeks out the assistance of an expert, whether that expert is a doctor, dentist, lawyer, accountant or plumber. The problem is that the consumer invariably is not well informed about whether the service is being provided properly.

To complicate the relationship further is the financial situation. In Canada, government financial restraints have affected every sector of public service, from education to defence to health care. As a result, many services are simply not available, or not available when they are needed or wanted. This has put an enormous amount of pressure on health facilities and the people who work in them. Doctors, nurses, health administrators and other health personnel are caught between an increasingly demanding public and a financial squeeze from government. Yet the patient is still legally entitled to a reasonable standard of care. The patient is also entitled to care provided according to the ethics of the various health professions.

These standards, however, are basic minimums. They do not include kindness, compassion, dignity or courtesy. One hopes that these standards will still apply even though it may be difficult to enforce them.

A further problem is that the health care system is a system of human beings, all of whom are different. No two nurses, physiotherapists or surgeons behave exactly the same or provide identical service. Some relate very well to some patients but not to others. Patients, too, are all different. They react differently to different people providing care and in their reaction to illness.

Should I Complain?

There are many areas of justifiable complaint. There are just as many areas where complaints are not justified. In an attempt to avoid the possibility of having to complain, the patient should become as well informed as possible. Insist upon being told whatever it is you want to know. Be open and honest. Do not fear punishment, abandonment or ridicule. Any health professional who refuses to answer questions or who suggests that the patient go elsewhere may not be worth having.

This also means that the patient must take on a certain amount of responsibility in working with health professionals. This includes providing complete and correct information, following instructions, asking questions about instructions, information or advice that is unclear or appears inappropriate. Patients have a responsibility for their own health.

Often complaints are not made because they may lead to confrontation and unpleasantness. Most people want to avoid such situations, especially if they are ill and feel dependent upon the person about whom they have a complaint. They also know that in many cases, complaining will do no good. An explanation will be given that will either justify or explain away the conduct. The defensive attitude of many health professionals and administrators may be used to justify their conduct and to prove to themselves that the complaint is groundless.

The more sophisticated health administrators regard all complaints as justified, in the sense that they want to have satisfied customers. They feel that an unsatisfied patient is one who often goes on to make an "unjustified" legal claim, which in itself can be disruptive and expensive to a health facility even if it is subsequently dropped. For this reason, more and more health facilities are becoming involved in risk management, which is designed to control the risk or potential liability or financial loss to the institution. Unfortunately, many facilities feel that as long as they improve the quality of care, they do not have to worry about risks. The result often is a growing number of dissatisfied patients, many of whom should never have been dissatisfied.

In making a complaint, the patient must clearly understand what the goal is, and choose the appropriate means. From the patient's point of view, the purpose of a complaint is often to gain an explanation, not to complain. Complaining for the sake of complaining achieves nothing.

Often a complaint arises out of a misunderstanding, or out of a reaction that was not expected, or from a failure of communication. In the emotion of mistreatment or misunderstanding, the matter has never been discussed with the person against whom the patient has a complaint. As difficult as it may be, the patient should make a diplomatic attempt to deal directly. Sometimes a family member or friend can assist. The point to be made is to try to calm the waters so that the matter does not escalate into an unnecessary confrontation. After the misunderstanding is over, the patient and the caregiver often must still work together.

Avenues of Complaint

If a direct complaint is not possible or does not achieve satisfactory results, there are other avenues of complaint. Each serves a different purpose. Often it may be necessary to choose more than one means, in order to achieve more than one result.

Complaints to the Institution

When the complaint is about an employee of an institution or a member of the medical staff, the complaint should be directed to the appropriate representative of the institution. This may also be necessary if the patient cannot identify the person against whom a complaint would be made.

In some cases the complaint can be made to the person's supervisor. However, the patient may not know who the supervisor is and cannot be expected to know the hospital hierarchy.

In most Canadian health institutions and health agencies, complaints should be directed to the top, to the administrator, who may carry the title chief executive officer, president or executive director. The complaint should include as much detail as possible with respect to dates, locations and personnel involved. If it does not deal with a particular event, but with the standard of service, details regarding the service and location should be included.

The administrator should bring the complaint to the attention not only of any physician involved but also of the medical director of the institution and the head of the relevant department.

If the complaint involves the conduct of a doctor, the complaint should be made directly to the chief executive officer of the institution. Hospitals have a set procedure in their by-laws for handling such complaints. The complaint should be investigated by a medical staff committee, which will make a recommendation. If the complaint is sufficiently serious, a physician could lose the privilege of practising medicine in the institution. This would require a decision of the hospital board. In some provinces, this action would automatically be reported to the provincial medical licensing authority, which could take action to suspend the doctor's licence.

In a long term care facility, the procedure is less complex, but complaints should also be made to the administrator.

If there is no response to a complaint made to the administrative head of the institution within a reasonable amount of time, a follow-up letter should be written to the chairman of the board with a copy to the administrator. If a response is still not received, legal advice should be considered.

In some hospitals and long term care facilities, there is a person called a patient representative, whose job it is to deal with complaints and to attempt to solve problems before they escalate into more serious matters. Some institutions may have a patient advocate or ombudsman who acts in a similar capacity.

Patients and families should be aware, however, that patient representatives are *not* representatives of patients. They are employees of the institution and represent the interests of the institution. This does not mean that they cannot be useful in resolving complaints. In fact, it is in the interests of the institution that patient complaints are settled, so that patients and their families do not take more serious and expensive action. In many institutions, patient representatives encourage patients to complain, or at least comment on the service, so that they do not leave feeling unhappy.

The patient representative acts as a mediator and has no power to correct anything that is amiss. Rather, the representative will take the patient's complaint to those who can correct the situation. If the complaint relates to an institutional procedure, the patient representative may be able to bring this to the attention of the administrator or executive director in order to find a solution. This does not prevent any patient or the family of any patient from complaining directly to the administrator. However, patient representatives can play a useful role in getting the machinery of the institution to run the way it is supposed to run, since they have the knowledge of the organization and the contacts, which the patient alone does not have.

Complaints to the Professional Authority

Most health professionals in Canada are either licensed or registered in the province or territory in which they work. In the case of most health professions such as medicine, dentistry and physiotherapy, a person cannot practise those professions or use the title of those professions without being licensed to do so. In many provinces registered nurses also must be licensed in practise. In other places, the registration gives them the right to use the title "registered" nurse.

Other health professions do not need a license to practise but do need to be registered in order to use the professional title.

Every professional licensing body has a system for receiving complaints and disciplining its members. This can include removing or suspending a licence or registration, which stops the person from practising their profession.

Professional discipline bodies do not have the same title throughout Canada. For example, in most provinces the body that has the authority to license and discipline physicians is called the College of Physicians and Surgeons. In Nova Scotia, however, it is the Provincial Medical Board.

Most provinces have two organizations for each profession. One is the professional association, which has no authority to discipline its members or to remove a member from practice. Although these organizations will often receive complaints and try to settle them, they exist to advance the interests of the members of that profession, not to protect the public. A licensing and disciplinary body, on the other hand, has as its purpose the protection of the public. It is important, therefore, that when a complaint is being made, it be made to the licensing authority. If a complaint is made to the professional association and can be settled amicably, so much the better, but the complainant should know that the association has no power to actually do anything.

In some professions, the licensing and the professional interest functions are carried out by the same organization. Increasingly, it is recognized that this places these organizations in a conflict of interest. One wonders how an organization can handle the complaint against a member when it also has the function of advancing the interests of the members, unless the discipline of a particular member in fact does that.

Complaints should always be directed to the provincial authority. National associations such as the Canadian Medical Association, the Canadian Nurses Association and the Canadian Dental Association have no authority to effectively discipline a member and remove that member from practice. Some of the national organizations do have discipline procedures in their by-laws, but the most that they can do is expel the member from the association.

The name and address of the appropriate provincial licensing and registration authority are available from the office of the provincial deputy minister of health and at most libraries. (Also see Appendix.)

Complaints to the Provincial Minister of Health
Since health is a provincial matter, it is pointless to complain to any federal authority for the acts of a health professional or a health facility, unless that facility operates directly under federal control. This would include any health service operated by Health Canada, the Department of National Defence or the Department of Veterans' Affairs. There are few facilities left in Canada operated by Veterans' Affairs; however, services are provided to veterans under contract with the department. The department does have responsibility for services that are provided on its behalf. Therefore, it is appropriate to complain to the Minister of Veterans' Affairs for services given to veterans through the department but in a regular hospital.

Complaints can also be made to the federal Solicitor General for health services provided by Corrections Canada in federal prisons, and to the Minister of Citizenship and Immigration for immigration health services. Because government departments are administered by deputy ministers, not ministers, most complaints should be sent to deputy ministers, rather than ministers, or at least with a copy to the deputy minister.

Complaints against a member of a particular health discipline directed to the provincial minister of health will invariably be referred to the appropriate registration or licensing body in the province. The comment may be made that the profession in question is "self-governing" and that the minister has no authority to interfere. Legally, that is correct. However, it must be remembered that a profession is self-governing because the province gave it that authority. If the profession is not exercising that authority appropriately, the government can remove that authority. Any complaint that arises in the legislature must be answered by the Minister of Health, who is responsible for health matters. The minister, therefore, can have extensive persuasive authority to ensure that the professional discipline body acts appropriately in response to public need.

In any complaint against a hospital, the matter will invariably be referred to the administrator of the institution. The provincial minister is again quite correct in making certain that the hospital authorities have the opportunity to correct the situation. However, if the hospital will not respond to the complaint or does not handle the matter properly, the minister has the duty to intervene.

Every hospital operates only with the authority of the provincial government through the minister of health. The minister, therefore, has an overall responsibility to ensure that certain standards are met.

In many cases the hospital is owned by the provincial government. The minister will not ordinarily become involved in the day-to-day operation of the facility, which usually functions in the same way as any private facility with an administrative head and a board. Once again, complaints to an institution that are not being handled properly by the institution itself may be referred to the minister.

To ensure that the minister responds to the complaint, it is sometimes advisable to refer the complaint to the minister through a local member of provincial legislature, or sometimes to send a copy to the leader of the opposition. However, the danger often is that the matter is then seen as a partisan political struggle, with considerations being taken into account that are not related to the complaint itself.

In the case of long-term-care facilities and home care agencies, some provinces deal with these matters under the department or ministry of health, whereas others license these agencies under the department or ministry of social or community services. Complaints to the minister must therefore be sent to the correct minister, or at least clearly identify the type of institution so that if it is sent to the wrong minister it may be correctly referred.

Many health services, particularly public health services, are often provided by municipalities. In these cases, complaints should be sent to the mayor, alderman or other elected official. It will then be referred to the correct administrative body, such as a board of health.

Complaints may also be sent to the provincial ombudsman. These officials do not have the power to correct a complaint but can bring pressure to bear on various authorities to handle it correctly. The ombudsman's office, however, does not always have the authority to deal with complaints affecting health services unless the services are directly part of government. The ombudsman's office can be very useful in directing the complaint to the correct authority and merely by becoming involved place additional pressure on whoever is responsible for handling the matter. Mental health services often have their own ombudsmen.

Complaints to Health Insurance Authorities

Frequently, complaints deal not with the standard of care but with the payment of services under the provincial health insurance plans. These complaints should be sent directly to the appropriate provincial authority that administers the plan. If the complaint concerns a physician accused of improperly billing the plan, a complaint may also be sent to the provincial medical disciplinary body.

The health insurance authorities have the power to remove the doctor from the plan and force the doctor to reimburse the plan for money that was improperly paid. The health insurance officials may also refer the matter to the provincial attorney general for consideration of prosecuting the doctor for a criminal offence.

Complaints to the Crown Prosecutor

Occasionally, an incident involving health personnel is so serious that it may amount to an offence under the Criminal Code of Canada. This might include fraud or sexual assault. A laboratory technician in Newfoundland was found guilty of criminal negligence for failing to cross-match blood, as a result of which a patient died.

It is possible for a citizen to launch a private prosecution, but this is a difficult task without legal representation and funds. A complaint to the Crown Prosecutor's office, however, may bring about a public prosecution if the prosecutors feel that there is sufficient evidence that an offence has taken place and that it can be proven. Full cooperation of the complainant is necessary, since the complainant will have to work closely with the Crown and be ready to be called as a witness in any trial. A potential witness should also be prepared to withstand vigorous cross-examination, in which the truth of the testimony will be questioned, as well as possibly the motivation, ethics and reliability of the witness. The complainant does not require legal counsel and would not be represented by a lawyer in court. The only reason for a witness to seek legal advice would be to determine whether there are any legal disadvantages to making a complaint to the Crown and to cooperating with the Crown as a witness.

At the end of a trial, even if a conviction results, the only satisfaction is that the accused is punished. The complainant gets no financial reward unless as part of the punishment some sort of restitution is ordered, though this is very unlikely.

Unless the offence is of a very sensitive nature, such as a sexual assault, and the judge agrees to have a closed court, the trial will be held in public with the press in attendance. Although Canadian trials are not televised as many are in the United States, and photographs may not be taken in the courtroom, those involved certainly may face the barrage of cameras outside the courthouse and the proceedings may be reported in the media.

A Lawsuit

The most widely discussed method of complaint is that of a patient launching a malpractice suit against the health professional or institution. (See chapter 22, "Why Don't Patients Sue?") It starts with an initial consultation with a lawyer. The lawyer should first of all be a trial lawyer — that is, a lawyer who is experienced and preferably specializes in trial work. If at all possible, the lawyer should be reasonably familiar with the health care system and be able to draw on medical experts. The difficulty is that the lawyers who are the most knowledgeable in health law often are retained by hospitals, the Canadian Medical Protective Association or insurers for health facilities.

It is technically possible for an individual to sue someone without having a lawyer, but this is not a recommended practice. They will have to be able not only to research the law on the subject but also to obtain medical or other consultants, analyse their advice and learn the often complicated rules of court proceedings. The risk of failure can be substantial. Without knowledge and experience in the malpractice field, it would also be very difficult to make a valid assessment of the merits of the case.

Of all of the avenues of complaint, a lawsuit is the only one that offers the patient the possibility of financial compensation for injuries. All other avenues of complaint are designed to either investigate or punish, but not to compensate. As a result, a lawsuit is also the only avenue that for all practical purposes requires the involvement of a lawyer. Therefore, it is also the only avenue of complaint that requires the patient to pay legal fees unless some sort of contingency arrangement can be entered into.

As in a criminal prosecution, the full cooperation of the patient (now plaintiff) is an absolute necessity. A great deal of time must be spent with the lawyer, and the patient must be prepared to be subjected to questioning not only by that lawyer but also by opposing lawyers in the discovery for examination sessions held outside a courtroom. (These proceedings are mainly to obtain more information in the hope that the parties can settle out of court.) If no settlement can be reached and the matter goes to trial, the patient must be prepared to be a witness. This will result in often aggressive cross-examination by opposing counsel, whose purpose is to show the judge and the jury (if there is one) that the patient's memory is so flawed that it cannot be relied upon, or that the patient is lying. A patient's credibility and motives may also come under attack.

If it is decided to proceed with a lawsuit, it must be done as quickly as possible, but at the same time not before all injuries are fully assessed. If the lawsuit is delayed for too long, it becomes more and more difficult to collect evidence, to find witnesses and to rely on the memory of witnesses.

There is also the problem of what is known as the statute of limitations, also referred to as the limitation period or the proscription period. This is the time during which a plaintiff is permitted to commence a lawsuit. Different time periods are established by each province for different types of lawsuits and often may depend on who is being sued. The limitation period ordinarily begins to run when the services complained of are concluded or, in some cases, when the injury is discovered. The period may be a year or two. It is often difficult to tell when the limitation period has begun to run and when it is over. Therefore, it is extremely important to receive legal advice as quickly as possible. To prevent the limitation period from expiring, it is often necessary to commence a lawsuit even though an out-of-court settlement may be a good possibility.

Complaints to the Coroner or Medical Examiner

If a person dies as a result of violence or from unknown causes or, in some provinces, in certain types of institutions such as a jail, the death comes within the authority of the coroner or, in Alberta, Manitoba and Nova Scotia, the medical examiner. The coroner or medical examiner may take control of the body, do an investigation into the death and conduct an autopsy. Deaths that may have been caused by negligence may also be investigated.

Even though the death may have occurred some time in the past, it is still possible to make a complaint to the local coroner or medical examiner. The result may be an investigation and a possible finding, though no compensation or punishment can be ordered.

Complaints to Other Officials and Organizations

Depending on the province and the situation, there may be other public officials to whom one can complain. It may be possible to complain to the provincial ombudsman, for example, if the complaint is about a government official or body or some other person or agency over whom the ombudsman has the power of investigation. The ombudsman does not have the authority to force correction, but can apply pressure to the body or agency in question and has the staff and ability to find its way through government bureaucracy.

If it is felt that a patient has suffered discrimination, as distinct from poor-quality care, on the basis of one of the criteria under provincial human rights legislation, such as race, physical disability or religion, a complaint can be made to the provincial human rights commission. This body has authority to investigate, hold hearings and take proceedings that can force compensation.

Some specialized organizations may assist in advising or assisting in patient complaints, such as the Psychiatric Patient Advocate Office of Ontario and the Canadian Mental Health Association at its various provincial branches. These organizations may be of particular value because they know the system and have the individual contacts, which can be very helpful in correcting a problem. They also have useful expertise or access to expertise. These associations also have persuasive authority with government that an individual acting alone would not have. However, private associations also have their own priorities and may be reluctant to intervene for a patient who is not considered high on the association's priority "wish list" in their dealings with government.

Complaints to the Media

Generally speaking, complaints to the media should be discouraged, for two reasons. The first is that if the complaint is designed to get action, help or cooperation, media coverage may antagonize the very people whose cooperation is sought. No person or institution that has been publicly embarrassed is going to be very welcoming in dealing with the patient who made the complaint.

The second reason is that once the patient goes to the media, the patient loses control. The complaint will not necessarily be put forward in media stories in the way the patient would like. The essence of the complaint may not even become the main story line.

However, often when no one is responding to the patient's complaints, media coverage can get machinery rolling. A medical disciplinary body that drags its feet in investigating a complaint, and a minister of health who refuses to put pressure on the disciplinary body, may often be forced to do something when the complaint hits the press.

It is often advisable to seek legal advice before going to the press, so that great care is taken in not jeopardizing any of the patient's legal rights such as the right to confidentiality. One cannot insist on confidentiality after attacking someone who has private information and who is forced to divulge it to make a public defence. Great care and often restraint must also be exercised in not committing defamation of anyone who might ordinarily have to respond to the complaint.

Rules of Complaint

It is important to know how to complain in order to get the best results and to correct the problem. Before any complaint is made, the patient must decide what is to be the goal. Is the complaint to correct an ongoing situation or to bring about an apology? Is it to correct action that has already been taken or to prevent action from being taken? Is it to simply record and gain recognition that a wrong has been committed, or is it to obtain monetary compensation? The method chosen to complain must be that which is most likely to achieve the desired result and not merely to let off steam. It should not antagonize those whose services may be required in the future, unless antagonism can produce effective results.

The following recommendations on how to complain may have to be modified to meet individual circumstances.

1. If a lawsuit is contemplated, seek legal advice before any complaint is made, since what is stated in a letter of complaint may jeopardize the success of the suit or any settlement negotiations. Once a lawyer has been retained, no letters or spoken comments, either in person or over the telephone, should be sent or made to anyone on the matter without first seeking the lawyer's advice.

2. Do not delay making a complaint. If too much time elapses, it may be difficult and sometimes impossible to investigate the complaint or to do anything about it.

3. Put the complaint in writing, sign it and date it.

4. Organize the letter in a point-by-point numbered form so that individual parts of it can be discussed, investigated and referred to easily. Do not let the complaint ramble on.

5. Refer to any previous oral complaints and conversations, specifically noting the person spoken to by name and position, the location and the dates.

6. Outline the facts as completely as possible, including the names and the positions (such as the admitting clerk) of the people involved, dates, times, and any identification numbers so that records of the circumstances can be traced. This is particularly important if the complaint involves an institution such as a hospital or out-patient clinic.

7. State specifically what action is being sought.

8. Insist that an investigation be undertaken and a written response be sent. If there is a response by telephone, ask that it be put in writing "for my files."

9. Do not request action that is outside the authority of the person or agency to whom the complaint is made. For example, if compensation is being sought, only a court can award it, which means that a lawyer should be consulted. If an investigation is being sought, other avenues are available.

10. Do not be vindictive. Ask for an investigation and particular action, not blood.

11. Set a reasonable date by which a response should be received. If a response has not been received when that time has elapsed, write again, asking what the status of the complaint is. Do not let the matter drag on for months. At some point, further action may be necessary through another authority to prompt a response.

12. If the letter is being sent to more than one person or agency, note on each copy the names of the persons to whom copies are being sent. Specifically note in the letter whether you are asking the others by copy to investigate as well. Some agencies attempt to coordinate their investigations to avoid duplication of effort. Others will do nothing until the others have completed their investigations.

13. Keep a copy of the complaint.

Summary of Principles
1. Complaints about the provision of health care should be made to the person or agency who has the authority to do something in response to the complaint.
2. Complaints should be made quickly, and in detail.
3. If the complaint seeks compensation, legal advice should be sought before the complaint is made.

WHY

DON'T

PATIENTS

SUE?

22

I N THE FIRST EDITION OF THIS BOOK, published in 1980, a chapter was included under the title "Why Do Patients Sue?" At that
time it was quite unusual for a patient to sue, or even to think
about suing, hospitals, doctors or dentists. This was something that
happened in the United States, not in Canada, where the British
North America Act (as Canada's constitution was then called) clearly
stated that Canada existed under the principle of "peace, order and
good government."

Canada still does not have the vast number of malpractice suits
or lawsuits that exist in the United States, but the number is certainly increasing. In fact, the situation has changed to such a degree that
the matter is now one of concern to the health system and the health
professions. It has also been of concern to government. In 1990, the
federal, provincial and territorial deputy ministers of health even
commissioned a special study into malpractice in Canada.

This change has taken place during a period when Canadians have placed less importance on peace, order and good government and become caught up with their "rights and freedoms" as given to them under the constitutional Charter of Rights and Freedoms. In this way Canada became more like the United States. Whether this shift in emphasis has anything to do with the growth of litigious activity is speculative.

The Canadian cultural atmosphere is also becoming more like that of the United States. Every American film, book, magazine article and television show dealing with law and lawsuits in that country is just as available to Canadians. The Canadian cultural industry mimics its American counterparts. The result is that Canadians, being subject to many of the popular cultural ideas of the United States, are bound to think and act more and more like Americans. If Americans like to sue their doctors, or each other, Canadians will tend to follow suit. The trend to medical malpractice suits is one indication.

The malpractice situation in this country is not nearly as serious as it is in the United States. In that country it is not unusual for some medical specialists to pay out more than $100,000 a year in malpractice insurance premiums. The threat of a malpractice suit in that country (and the high premiums for insurance) has helped to create a number of problems.

It has discouraged physicians from entering high-risk specialties and from practising in high-risk states. Not all specialities are at the same risk of malpractice suits, and risks vary widely across the country. The risk of a doctor being sued in California is far greater than for a doctor in a similar practice in Vermont. An obstetrician is more likely to be sued than an allergist or dermatologist.

This does not mean that California doctors are not as good as Vermont doctors, or that obstetricians are not as good as dermatologists. It simply means that the patients in one part of the United States are more litigious than another, and that the patients of one branch of medicine are more likely to sue than patients of another.

The American situation has also encouraged the development of various insurance alternatives to that of private malpractice carriers. This has been a result of both the difficulty of obtaining private insurance and the high cost. Various doctor-owned protective groups have been started, similar to the approach taken by the Canadian Medical Protective Association and the Medical Defence Union and Medical Protective Society in Britain.

This movement towards a more litigious society is not simply the usual delayed Canadian reaction to an American development. It is a development that is taking place throughout the developed world. Great Britain, Ireland, Australia, Israel and Sweden are among those countries that have seen similar developments.

In fact, when one looks at the millions of medical and other health care procedures that take place in Canada every year, there are amazingly few lawsuits brought by patients. One would like to think that the reason is that Canadians are receiving reasonably good health care services, or at least that they are more or less satisfied with the services they are receiving. This is probably true.

Even with what appears to be the eventual collapse of the health insurance and financing system as Canadians have known it, so far the level of service in most cases has been reasonably good. At least Canadians who are not completely happy with it have not been prepared to complain.

There is no way an accurate measurement can be made of how many Canadians are dissatisfied with the particular care they have received from particular people or institutions from time to time. We do know that there are more claims for compensation, more lawsuits and more complaints to professional disciplinary bodies than ever before. There is also a feeling among lawyers and others that there are thousands upon thousands of Canadians who have on occasion been very unhappy with the health services they have received. Most of these Canadians did nothing about it. Some may have made an oral complaint to someone. They may even have consulted a lawyer, but they never actually started a lawsuit. This does not mean that they could not have won their suits or that the basis for the complaints was not legally justified. It simply means that they did not make use of the legal mechanism to pursue their complaints against the health care system.

One could speculate that every complaint that is received by a disciplinary body or every claim against a hospital or nursing home represents many more unhappy consumers who are silent. It is presumed, similarly, that each letter received by a member of Parliament represents many other voters who have not written. But unfortunately, many who work in the administration of the health care system judge patient satisfaction on the basis of the few complaints. Many administrators and health planners believe that if the quality of care can be maintained or even improved, this in itself will contain the threat of lawsuits and complaints. Anyone in the claims business knows that this is both naive and untrue. Unhappiness exists even with the best of care. Furthermore, the quality of the care received by the patient does not mean that the legal rights of the patient have been respected. The question that must be asked, therefore, is why more patients whose legal rights have not been respected, or who believe that their rights have not been respected, do not take legal action.

Large Court Awards

American commentators have for many years blamed the generosity of their courts for encouraging malpractice suits. The money awarded by courts, which was then reflected in out-of-court settlements, was so large that disgruntled patients were encouraged to try for the pot of gold at the end of the rainbow. The prospect of highly publicized awards in the millions of dollars for "pain and suffering" and "mental anguish" seemed to make the gamble of a lawsuit worthwhile.

It is a difficult problem facing any court to put a price tag on someone's injury. What is the dollar value of a paralysed arm, a blinded eye or a death? Is it "worth" the same for everyone? Is the amputated leg worth the same for a clerk who sits at a desk all day, for a surgeon who stands or for an elderly person who no longer is supporting a family and has an adequate pension? What is the loss of a human life worth, especially if life insurance gives to the family more than if the deceased was alive?

In a lawsuit, the plaintiff can seek only one thing — money. That is the purpose of a medical malpractice case. The court can order the defendant only to pay money to the plaintiff. The paralysed body, the aching back, the lost kidney cannot be repaired or replaced. An exact money figure must be placed on the injury.

The special damages, which can be calculated exactly, are clear-cut. They are the actual expenses incurred as a result of the injury, such as uninsured medical or nursing care costs, or lost income. In addition, future expenses must be determined. This largely depends on a calculated guess of how long the plaintiff might live and what those expenses are likely to be. If a person is to remain in a nursing home until death, actuaries will calculate the number of years and what the cost of that care is likely to be over the years. It may turn out that the calculations are incorrect and the losing defendant may have paid out too much or not enough. However, the plaintiff gets only one kick at the can. The award once given, and after the time allowed for appeal has elapsed, is fixed forever.

The more difficult sum to set is that of general damages, which include the loss of enjoyment of life for a person who is now paralysed or suffers from an incurable disease; the loss of years of life; the pain, the suffering and the torment; the loss of companionship and the loss of marital relations. There is no scientific method of determining what these are worth in dollars and cents. It is simply a guess on the part of the judge or a jury. Such guesses are largely governed by what the courts have awarded in similar cases and by how those making these decisions feel about it. Their feelings will be affected by their social, cultural and religious attitudes. The only guidelines will be the very broad limits that have been laid down in previous cases.

A number of years ago, the Supreme Court of Canada attempted to keep Canadian awards from getting out of hand, so that these general damages have not reached the huge amounts reported in the United States. Despite these attempts, Canada has seen awards of more than $1 million. The size, however, is usually attributable not to general damages but to the cost of future care, especially if a plaintiff requires institutional care for the rest of his or her life.

Whether high injury awards encourage malpractice lawsuits may be so in the United States, but it is not likely the case in Canada. The amounts given here are still too low, although this may be changing in cases of very serious injuries that are "worth" a lot of money.

What It Costs to Sue

In the United States, doctors frequently blame lawyers for provoking lawsuits by what has been called the contingent fee system of billing. This billing system finances most malpractice suits in the United States. Until recently it was largely prohibited in Canada.

The traditional way of paying a lawyer is similar to the traditional way of paying any other person who provides a service. The service is provided and a bill is rendered, on the basis of either a set fee for that service or an hourly rate. The fees are set either by the provider of the service or by a professional governing body. The fees are based not on value but on what consumers are willing to pay and what the provider of the service would like to earn. In the case of legal services, it is quite common for a lawyer to charge different clients different fees on the basis of what the lawyer thinks the client will or can pay and what the service might be "worth" to that particular client.

The contingent fee system is based solely on whether the lawyer is successful in obtaining the compensation sought by the client. The lawyer and the client enter into a contract in which the lawyer is to charge a percentage (usually 25 percent or more) of the amount collected either through negotiation and out-of-court settlement or by a court award after litigation. In the United States the legal fees for medical malpractice are commonly as high as 40 percent and sometimes even as high as 50 percent. Legislative controls continue to be suggested.

In some cases, the lawyer absorbs out-of-pocket expenses, in other cases the client pays these, in still others these costs may be shared. These costs include not only the salaries of other lawyers working on a case but also the fees and expenses of the medical or other experts who must be hired to advise the lawyer and to review the evidence.

In 1973 the Secretary's Commission on Medical Malpractice in the United States found that the contingent fee system did not in fact encourage people to start lawsuits. This accusation was based on the belief that since the client had nothing to lose, there was nothing to stop a lawsuit. Therefore, a lawsuit could easily be started on the basis of the most frivolous of complaints.

This assumption ignores the position of the lawyer. Since the lawyer is going to be working without the certainty of getting paid, such a case will be undertaken only if the lawyer thinks that there is a very good chance of winning, and if the amount that could be collected makes it worthwhile to put in what might be a great deal of work in order to share in that amount.

The result may be that lawyers will take on only those cases that have a good chance of success. Cases that may be just as meritorious but more difficult to prove will have a lesser chance of attracting counsel. Lawyers may also be willing to take on cases that can be pursued at the early stages without much work or expense, but not if the going gets rough.

The contingent fee system in fact discourages small lawsuits in which the client should be compensated but the injury would not attract a large award, which does not make it worthwhile for a lawyer to take the case.

However, many American doctors still believe that the number of lawsuits is largely generated by the contingent fee system. Many Canadian doctors also held such a belief for many years even though the system was not generally used in Canada. In most provinces a lawyer could be disbarred for using it, on the grounds that the lawyer's advice and conduct must be objective and not influenced by what the lawyer may personally gain from the success of the case.

However, the contingent fee system is now permitted in most provinces, though the rates charged are tightly controlled and it is subject to supervision by the courts. Despite these changes, most Canadian lawyers prefer not to take on cases on this basis because of the risks of not getting paid. Many simply do not take cases that in their opinion are worth less than a satisfactorily high amount. All other cases would have to be dealt with in the usual manner, that being fee for service with certain amounts payable in advance.

The result is that the legal profession actually discourages lawsuits because for most people the costs of litigation are too high. Many lawyers are reluctant to even speculate on the costs of a potential trial and a possible appeal. When a trial may cost $50,000 to $100,000, compared to compensation of that amount or less, it is obvious that a lawsuit is not worth the money for most people.

In addition, the costs to the lawyer can be high. To even begin an investigation of a case, experts will have to be found to review the patient's records. The experts may be so expensive that the client cannot even proceed to this stage. Even finding experts may be expensive and time consuming, since in the less-populated areas of Canada where doctors all know each other, it may be difficult to get one doctor to comment on the actions of another. This may be looked at by lawyers as a particularly frustrating attitude, but one must remember that after the malpractice suit has come and gone, the doctors must still get along and work with each other.

The Legal Come-on

In the United States, advertising by lawyers in the press and on television is designed to encourage unhappy patients to become clients and at least see whether their rights have been breached and whether they could be compensated. A standard advertisement will read:

> **"Injured? We'll make everyone at fault pay.**
> *** Auto Accidents * Medical Malpractice ***
> *** Slip & Fall * Brain Damage * Work Injuries ***
> **Call the injury lawyer.**
> **Home and hospital appointments."**

A few years ago such an advertisement in Canada would have resulted in swift professional discipline. Advertising still raises eyebrows among the more conservative members of the bar. However, lawyers are gradually beginning to use marketing and advertising to promote themselves. Many Canadian law firms now produce the most elegant and "tasteful" brochures to attract clients.

There is no doubt that more people are suing than ever before. There are more lawyers than ever, which means more legal work — and litigation — will be produced, just as when more surgeons are available, there is more surgery.

The Jury System

In the United States, almost all malpractice cases are heard before a civil jury. In Canada, most are heard only before a judge. It has been suggested by some that the jury system encourages lawsuits, because juries are assumed to be more compassionate to the injured patient than to the defendant doctor or hospital. There is absolutely no evidence that this is true. A jury may be more sympathetic to a doctor who is hard working and dedicated and being sued by an aggressive, hypochondriac patient.

The Cost of Injury

When people are injured and place the blame on someone else, they ordinarily do not want to sue. What they usually want is to be protected from out-of-pocket expenses. They are not looking for compensation for pain and suffering, which they will accept as one of those unfortunate experiences of life.

In Canada, under the provincial health insurance plans there are very few medical or hospital expenses that are not paid for. Only services such as home care, long term care and semi-private or private hospital care are not covered. The result is that most people who are injured in Canada are not out of pocket. If there are no additional expenses, and no long term injuries, the motivation to sue is much diminished.

In the United States, it is argued that since so many people are uninsured or not completely insured, there is a stronger incentive to seek compensation for costs, with compensation for general damages being added. This proposition has not been proven and remains speculative.

Malpractice Insurance

It can be argued that malpractice insurance encourages patients to sue. The patient knows that the doctor, the dentist or the institution is insured, so any compensation will come from a large insurance company rather than from an individual or institution. The patient has the impression that no harm will take place and that a lawsuit will not financially punish those who provided the care.

For this reason some American doctors "go bare" and practise without insurance. They advertise this fact to their patients as if to say, "Sue me. I don't have any money." Personal financial resources are transferred to someone else for protection.

In Canada, most doctors are members of the Canadian Medical Protective Association (CMPA), with some being privately insured. Many hospitals require their medical staff to be CMPA members or to carry private insurance. All institutions carry insurance. The result is that for many Canadian physicians, "going bare" is not possible.

The availability of what is perceived to be a large pot of money has been countered in Canada by the very conservative defence attitude of the CMPA, which takes a different attitude towards claims than do private insurance companies. Private insurers, which are established to make a profit, are invariably guided by financial considerations. Quite apart from the merits of a claim, payments may be made by private insurers because it is cheaper to settle the claim than to spend enormous sums on legal fees for a comparatively small claim. Claims may also be settled because of the difficulties of defending them with poor witnesses or poor evidence. On the other hand, if the claim is substantial, an insurance company may balk at settling in the hope that the claimant's financial resources and energy will eventually be exhausted, even though the claim may have merit.

The Canadian Medical Protective Association is not an insurance company. It is an organization of doctors established to defend its members who are sued for medical malpractice. There are no policies issued, and no limits on the amounts that can be paid out, unlike under an insurance policy. The theory is that its decisions are based solely on the merits of a claim and not on financial considerations, since it is a non-profit organization. If a claim has merit, it will be settled. If it has none, it will be defended regardless of what it might cost to defend it.

In fact, the CMPA has developed a reputation among many lawyers in Canada for its purported mandate to defend its members at all costs regardless of the merits of the claims. This may be sour grapes on the part of many losing plaintiffs' lawyers. However, the impression is that CMPA solicitors will use every technicality to delay and to beat down an opponent rather than to settle.

This impression seems to be sufficiently widespread that many lawyers advise patients who are thinking of suing that CMPA will be a formidable opponent. Whether this discourages lawsuits against

Canadian doctors is difficult to determine, but it certainly has not made it easy to make claims of questionable merit against doctors.

None of these arguments apply to claims against hospitals, nursing homes, home care agencies and other health professionals, for which the private insurance industry dominates either totally or in combination with various self-insurance schemes.

It is interesting to note that the Medical Defence Union, of London, England, which has medical and dental members all over the world, will not accept members in Canada or the United States. The MDU pulled out of Canada some years ago when it was felt that the costs of defending claims in this country and the awards and settlements were escalating at such a rate that the number of Canadian members was not able to support them. The situation since the MDU departure has in fact worsened for the medical profession, and the CMPA has not been able to contain the problem.

Doctor–Patient Relations

As a general rule, people do not like suing each other. They particularly do not like suing people with whom they have a good relationship. Litigation, the courts and involvement with lawyers are generally regarded as nasty, disreputable activities. Despite the propaganda put out by the Canadian Bar Association and the various provincial bars, lawyers as a group do not have a good reputation with much of the population. They see criminals going free because of a good lawyer who wins on a technicality. They see judges who appear to hold their positions as a political reward, even though enormous strides have been made to clean up the method of judicial appointments. They hear of lawyers milking their clients with highly questionable results, and they hear of splashy downtown offices from which enormous power is generated. To consult one's solicitor is not something the average Canadian does lightly.

As a result, most patients who have become closely involved with their doctors are loath to sue, even if there is obviously negligence, quite apart from a mere suspicion of negligence. In small communities, people do not sue their local hospital, since it is theirs. They have served on the board or the auxiliary and their friends are involved in its activities. It is a part of their lives and one of the foundations of their community. In many communities the hospital is the major source of employment.

However, the health care system is changing. More and more medical care is given on referral to specialists in larger centres who see the patient so briefly that no personal relationship is established. Because of the sophisticated facilities and staff that are now required, fewer procedures are being performed in small hospitals. Many small hospitals across Canada either have become long term care facilities or have given up doing surgery and obstetrics. Patients are instead transferred to regional hospitals to be treated by physicians they have never met. In these circumstances it is much more difficult to establish a close personal relationship, and if something does go wrong, the patient does not have the same hesitancy about commencing legal action.

The growing tendency to provide care, and particularly care in which the risks are significant, in these impersonal situations increases the possibility of lawsuits. One cannot say that it encourages lawsuits, but it does remove the social impediments to a lawsuit.

Patient Expectations

Ever since World War II, advances in medicine have been miraculous. These advances have been given wide publicity in the popular press and on television. Financial campaigns to raise money for health care institutions and health associations have inundated the public with the message that with enough time, effort and money everything is possible. Every illness, every disease, can be controlled, can be cured. Everyone wants to hear of the latest miracle.

Experimental developments are widely reported in the press, even though they may never lead to successful medical treatments, or at least not for many years.

The proliferation of health disciplines has also boosted this climate of optimism. The traditional disciplines and the new folks on the block all try to capture the public's attention and admiration through their public relations efforts. They are all helping to make a better world.

Failures, too, are put forward in a positive light. The image is that despite all of the best efforts made, the patient died. Even those involved in palliative care look at dying as a "positive" experience. Those promoting suicide view it positively.

There is no doubt that health professionals are oriented towards making people better — as it should be. And they want the patient to be part of this positive mind-set, since it is felt that a patient with a positive attitude has a much better chance (in most circumstances) of getting better. The attitude is that one should never take away hope.

Those attitudes and approaches cannot be condemned out of hand, though on many occasions their proponents do get carried away. However, the result is that North Americans now have enormous expectations of their health care system, expectations that far outstrip the realities. They have heard of the miracles, the developments, the cures, and they want them now for their personal problems and for their friends and relatives.

When these expectations are not met, there is a feeling that the patient did not get what was deserved and available. It must have been someone's fault. Someone must have made a mistake. Someone must have been negligent. This feeling encourages complaints, litigation and claims. The seeds of a lawsuit are sown.

Added to this is the negative publicity generated by medical societies complaining about low incomes, which are in fact far in excess of average Canadians'. Even though doctors work longer hours than average Canadians, have the expenses of running an office and spend many more years in school, seeing doctors acting like line workers on strike at an automobile assembly plant destroys the mystique. It has helped to remove medicine from its cultural and social position that patients felt uncomfortable about criticizing, let alone suing. In this way, medicine had shared a protected position along with the church and the Queen.

Only in America
As already noted, the public constitutional atmosphere in Canada is moving closer to that of the United States, where there is a greater interest in personal rights and freedoms than in peace, order and good government. This does not mean that every American has the rights that the law and Constitution supposedly guarantee, but at

least most Americans think they do. Traditionally, Canadians did not think they had such rights even though they did.

American political and cultural traditions reinforced this mentality. From early school years throughout life, Americans hear all sorts of propaganda about liberty, justice and writing to their congressmen. The result has been a belief that if an American thinks something is wrong, someone can be done about it, and someone ought to pay. The legal profession aggressively encourages Americans to seek legal advice and to take action, thus creating a litigious atmosphere.

Canada, on the other hand, is a country based on compromise, and Canadians tend to accept situations they do not like in order to preserve peace. They are therefore less ready to fight for their rights.

The Difficulty in Suing

The primary reason that more unhappy patients do not sue in Canada is that the law places such a heavy burden on the plaintiff that the odds and costs of winning discourage most people who consider it. The care the patient received may have been substandard and even sloppy. The patient may have been injured as a result of the treatment, or did not get better. None of these facts are sufficient to win a lawsuit.

The first hurdle that a plaintiff must overcome is that the burden of proof is on the plaintiff. It is the plaintiff who must prove to the satisfaction of the court that *negligence* took place, not sloppy care, not incompetenence, and not injury. (See chapter 5, "Negligence and Standards of Care.") This burden is achieved by the plaintiff being able to present evidence of all the actions that make up negligence. It is the plaintiff who must convince the court by use of witnesses and experts that the care fell below the average, reasonable and prudent standard in the circumstances and that the injury not only occurred but was reasonably foreseeable. To do this is time consuming and very expensive. The defendant will also have experts, who will disagree with the plaintiff's experts. Unless the plaintiff's experts are very convincing, it becomes a gamble as to whether the court will accept the plaintiff's case over the defendant's.

A complaint against the care or treatment does not amount to proving that negligence occurred. It is possible that the care was poor but did meet the minimum standard. The law does not require *good* care and treatment, only care and treatment that meets the bare minimum. Even if the care did not meet the minimum standard, the plaintiff may not be able to bring forward experts who can say that the injury was a reasonably foreseeable result.

These many difficulties stand in front of a plaintiff searching for a successful lawsuit and compensation. A good lawyer will fully advise the patient of this, and in most cases will discourage the patient from proceeding. Even on a contingency basis, lawyers will refrain from suing because the chances of success are so small. This is probably the greatest impediment to lawsuits.

The Trauma of a Lawsuit

Even if finances are not an issue and legal counsel feels that the various hurdles can be overcome, there remains the trauma of a lawsuit. Even before any formal legal proceedings begin, the patient, who has already suffered the emotional trauma of the injury and its aftereffects, will be required to have extensive meetings with legal counsel. These meetings will require the patient to relive in minute detail events that may be very painful to remember. The patient will be subjected to questioning, and at times feel that the lawyer does not believe the story.

Once formal proceedings begin, what are called discovery proceedings may be held with the defendant's lawyer, during which the patient-turned-plaintiff is placed under attack, though not in a courtroom. Finally, the trial takes place, in which every aspect of the plaintiff's case will be subject to doubt. The patient's motives, credibility and even ethics may be placed under attack. The patient may be pictured as ungrateful to those who have dedicated themselves to the restoration of health and life. Each of these steps will be preceded with further briefings with legal counsel, going over and over again circumstances that may be painful to relate.

Few individuals can withstand such pressures without some strain. These factors alone discourage most people from taking legal action, regardless of how legally justified their complaint may be.

Summary of Principles

1. Patients make a decision to sue or not to sue, not on the legal merits of their case or whether they are legally entitled to be compensated for their injures, but on whether they feel a wrong has been done.

2. Patients rarely sue unless there has been an actual injury or a failure to respond to treatment.

3. Patients usually do not sue a doctor or other health professional when there has been a close personal relationship.

4. It is highly speculative as to what does or does not motivate patients to take legal action against their caregivers, though an injury, the failure to have expectations fulfilled and a breakdown in the relationship between the patient and the caregiver are certainly important motivators, along with a heightened awareness of legal rights.

5. Medical malpractice suits are difficult, time consuming and expensive to win, and as a result most of them are either discontinued or lost.

23

DYING

AND

DEATH

HOW OFTEN HAVE CLERGYMEN, philosophers and medical scientists asked, "What is death?" People have speculated and theorized since the beginning of recorded time and yet the speculation continues. In the meanwhile, in order to make daily decisions respecting patients, some sort of practical definition must be used. Because we think we know what life is, death is usually defined as the cessation of life. The cessation of life has traditionally been defined as the final cessation of vital functions, such as breathing and heartbeat.

In the past this was never a problem. You were dead when a doctor declared that you were dead. When the Church said you were dead, you were definitely dead. Yet because modern technology permits these vital functions to be kept going after death, the definition of death may not be as exact as it once was.

It is not always possible to determine whether a person is dead. Because of this uncertainty, medicine often looks to the law for a definition. Death, however, is not a legal matter. It is a fact to be determined by those who are trained to diagnose conditions of the body, namely physicians. The law gets involved when there is a dispute over facts and a court must decide what the facts were at a particular time. In other words, the issue is whether or not someone was dead at a particular time.

The law also becomes involved in determining the legal consequences of death. The law examines whether the legal rights and duties of various individuals change when someone dies.

Does Death Matter?

It does matter when a person dies, for a number of legal reasons. When a person dies, all civil rights that person had immediately vanish. The dead have no rights at all, though in some cases others take on those rights, such as the executors of an estate. The person who is dead can no longer start a lawsuit, nor be sued. Only the representative of the estate of the deceased can sue or be sued. The estate comes into existence at the moment of the person's death.

When alive, a person can buy and sell property and run up debts. As soon as death occurs, only the estate can carry on these activities, and then only subject to any restrictions in the person's will, the discretion granted to the executors in the will and any provincial statutes governing estates.

Whether a person is alive or dead may affect a claim against the estate. If Uncle Joe leaves $5,000 to his sister's child Sally, unless Sally dies before he does (in which case it goes to his landlady, Mrs. P), it is very important to know if Sally was alive when Uncle Joe died. If she was not, Mrs. P gets the money. If she was alive but has since died, Sally's estate gets it and distributes it according to her will. Usually it is quite clear whether Sally was or was not alive when Uncle Joe died. If, however, Sally had slipped into a coma and had her breathing and heartbeat maintained by mechanical means, during which time Uncle Joe died, was she alive at that time? Did she die before he did? After Uncle Joe's death, the machines were turned off and Sally stopped breathing and her heart stopped. At that time she was definitely dead, but was she in fact already dead? Who gets the money? It all depends on the moment of death.

The question also arises in malpractice situations. A person is injured in an automobile accident as a result of the negligence of another driver. The victim is taken to hospital and placed on life supports. Due to negligence in the hospital, life supports are removed and all vital functions cease. The estate takes action against the driver of the other motor vehicle. The defence is that, although there may have been negligence, the death was actually caused by the hospital. The estate alleges that in fact the patient was already dead when life supports were applied. If that was the case, the death was due to the driver, not to the negligence of the hospital staff. The issue then is to determine when the patient had died.

The problem also arises in criminal cases. Jack assaults Luke. Luke is seriously injured and is taken to hospital unconscious. His breathing and heartbeat are maintained mechanically. After numerous consultations, it is decided to turn off all equipment. The consensus among the medical consultants is that there is no hope for recovery. The equipment is turned off and the heartbeat and respiration stop. Did Luke just die, or has he been dead for some time? If he was already dead, Jake may be convicted of murder, or perhaps manslaughter. If Luke was not dead, Jake could argue that the hospital killed him and that the death was not inevitable. He may, therefore, be guilty of a lesser charge. Such an argument is unlikely to succeed, but a great deal of time and effort may be spent advancing it. Section 225 of the Criminal Code of Canada has taken much of the weight out of this defence by stating that if a person injures another and death results, he is said to have caused the death of the victim even though the actual cause of death was treatment that was given in good faith after the injury occurred.

Of all the problems arising from whether or not a person is dead, the most common relates to the transplantation of vital organs. A patient whose vital organs are being maintained artificially may be a prime candidate as a donor of a heart, say, which may be in very good health. Obviously, vital organs cannot be removed if the patient is alive. On the other hand, if vital organs are left in a dead body, they too will die and be useless for transplantation. It is absolutely necessary to know, therefore, whether the person is alive or dead at the time the transplantation is to take place. Even though breathing and circulation are maintained for the transplantation, the donor must be dead.

When Does Death Occur?

Traditionally, death occurred when a physician said that all vital functions had ceased. At that time, however, physicians were able to determine only the vital signs of respiration and heartbeat. In the vast majority of cases, this is still the way death (and the time of death) is determined.

It is now recognized that many other non-vital bodily functions continue after these two functions have ceased. Fingernails and hair continue to grow for a number of hours after the rest of the body has died. The body dies over a period of time, although few would argue that the person is still alive until everything has ceased.

How many bodily functions have to cease before we can truly say that death has occurred? In modern times it has been realized that one of the most important bodily functions is that of the brain. Medical science has now said that if the brain continues to function, the person is alive. Similarly, if the brain has ceased to function, the person is truly dead. This is referred to as brain death.

Brain death is determined by measuring the electrical impulses of the brain with an electroencephalograph (EEG). There is some disagreement about how long there must be a flat EEG tracing, which shows absence of brain activity, before a doctor can say that a person has died, and what level of brain activity must have ceased.

Because of these disagreements, some in the medical community have looked to the law to give guidance. But death is not a legal matter. It is a medical diagnosis. It is a conclusion drawn by those learned in medical science. To ask lawyers, politicians and judges to set criteria upon which doctors would determine a diagnosis would be strange indeed.

A further problem would be that as scientific knowledge about what constitutes death changes, it would be necessary to use the political legislative process to change the law to meet current scientific realities. One would have the spectacle of people lobbying legislators to pass a law that certain facts exist or do not exist, quite apart from what scientists and medical researchers believe. This would be a return to the days when there were laws stating that the earth was flat. Scientific development would have to be suppressed until the political process was able to have the law changed.

As a result, the law has generally not become involved in Canada. Manitoba has passed legislation to allow for the acceptance of brain death as a determining factor. It does not require that brain death always be used, however.

Death, therefore, is a matter of fact and not of law. If the issue arises as to whether a person is dead, it is to be determined in the same way as any other matter of fact before a court. Medical experts would state whether they thought the person was dead at a particular time. They would be asked how that was determined. The experts may disagree. The court must then decide which experts are to be believed.

What bothers doctors is that they may make a mistake and take action on a patient who they thought was dead but in fact was not. They may remove a vital organ from a patient who was alive. They may refrain from treating a patient in the belief that the patient was dead. This will always be a problem. A court can always declare that the decision of the doctor was negligent. Similarly, decisions of lawyers, accountants and garage mechanics are subject to scrutiny by the courts. To ask the law to make decisions ahead of time, however, removes the ability of physicians to exercise professional judgement, which is what they are trained to do. The law would bind doctors in making professional judgements even when their scientific knowledge tells them to decide otherwise.

Legislation that defines death will not, therefore, assist the advancement of medical practice, nor will it enhance the rights of patients and their families.

Occasionally, one reads or hears that a court has accepted brain death as the law. In fact, nothing of the sort has happened. It simply means that the court has accepted the testimony of a witness who has stated that using the latest medical definition of death, the person in question was dead. The court merely accepted an expert opinion on what the facts were. The method of determining those facts was the current practice, that of brain death. In a number of years, if a new method is developed, the courts will accept that. In this way the law follows changes in medical and scientific knowledge, rather than imposing solutions that are inflexible and soon become archaic.

Is There a Right to Die?

The media constantly raise the issue of whether there is a right to die. The title of the play "Whose Life Is It, Anyway?" has sounded a rallying call for the forces of the right-to-die movement. The fact is that there is no right to die. However, it is not that simple and there is a great deal of uncertainty. There is also an ethical debate, which infringes on the legal issues and complicates any discussion of the issue.

Despite the confusion and wide publicity given to American cases and the famous Quebec case of *Nancy B.*, a number of answers are falling into place. They are doing so largely because of a change in public attitude and a few court cases. Canadians do not usually solve these legal and ethical dilemmas by running to the courts. The attitudes of hospitals and doctors have been changing, and as a result the practice relating to death and dying has also been changing.

Is There a Right to Live?

If there is no right to die, is there a right to live? The answer is yes, but even that is not absolute. The basic rights that are applied to death and dying are exactly the same as in any other situation. The first is that there is a right to average, reasonable and prudent medical care. Ordinarily, care that is average, reasonable and prudent is designed to prevent reasonably foreseeable injury or death. The patient has a right to care that attempts to preserve life.

This does not mean that everything conceivable must be done to preserve life. It means that everything that the average, reasonable and prudent doctor or hospital would do in the circumstances to preserve life must be done. If certain procedures, even if they would preserve life, are generally regarded as not reasonable in the circumstances, the patient has no right to them.

Ordinarily, if a patient's heart or breathing stops, the reasonable response is to attempt resuscitation to revive the patient. However, if the patient is severely ill, or very elderly, it may be that resuscitation could not be sustained. Even though the patient could be resuscitated, another respiratory or cardiac arrest is likely to occur, and another and another. The question then is whether resuscitation is appropriate considering the pain of the patient from the procedure and the likelihood that the procedure will have only a temporary result. There is no legal right, therefore, to what is referred to as extraordinary care, especially care that is unreasonable given the circumstances of the patient.

Even though the failure to provide certain procedures results in death, that in itself does not give the patient the legal right to those procedures. The question is always whether those procedures are reasonable for that patient in that patient's circumstances.

Ordinarily, because resuscitation must take place promptly, there is no time to weigh the pros and cons of doing it. However, because these situations can often be predicted, if a decision not to resuscitate is made, "DNR" is written on the patient's chart. This means "Do Not Resuscitate." In the past various euphemisms were used, including "No Code Blue" and "No Code 99." As long as it was reasonable not to resuscitate in the circumstances, the patient had no legal right to resuscitation, and the subsequent death could not be claimed as wrongful by the survivors.

This right or rather lack of it, can be applied to many other circumstances involving death. For example, many nursing homes will place a "DNH" order on the chart, or "Do Not Hospitalize." If the resident becomes acutely ill, no transfer is to take place to a hospital, even though that is what ordinarily would take place. In the particular circumstances, it may not be reasonable to do that, since hospitalization will not be of any benefit. What may be reasonable is care and comfort.

These principles apply equally to numerous situations, such as the decision to carry out surgery, to tube feed or to place a patient on a respirator. Even though many of these procedures may save a life or prolong it, other considerations may not make such a decision reasonable in the circumstances.

It is on these principles that palliative care has developed. In a palliative care program, a dying patient is made as comfortable as possible. No treatment is given that would ordinarily be used to prolong life. Measures would also be used, such as various medications to alleviate pain, that may hasten death but in the circumstances are considered reasonable. What is considered reasonable has changed over time, so that the reluctance to give a narcotic liberally on the grounds that it is addictive has now disappeared. Since the patient is dying, it hardly matters whether the patient becomes addicted; what is important is that the patient be kept as comfortable and as pain-free as possible.

The Right to Refuse Care, and the Living Will

Even though the patient does not have the legal right to die, there is always the legal right to refuse care or treatment. (See chapter 4, "Consent to Treatment.") Any procedure, medication or surgery may be refused for whatever reason, even though the refusal may result in the patient's death. This fundamental legal right exists even when the patient is dying.

The Ontario Court of Appeal made it very clear, in the case of *Malette v. Shulman,* that every person has the right to refuse care. The court said that Mrs. Malette had the right to refuse a blood transfusion, even though without it she would die.

Quebec also made it clear in the case of *Nancy B.* that a patient who was being kept alive by a respirator had the right to refuse continued use of the device, even though she would die as a result. She was not dying at the time of her refusal.

In both cases, there was no right to die. The right was to refuse care or treatment regardless of the consequences.

Various issues have been raised by American courts that have not yet come up in Canada but upon which one could speculate. If a pregnant woman required surgery to save her life, would she have the right to refuse care, since such refusal would result in her death, or the death of the foetus, or both? Since Canadian law does not recognize a foetus as a human being, even though there are certain legal duties towards it, it would be very doubtful that the right to refuse care or treatment would be removed from the woman.

With this background, it is clear that Canadians can have what are popularly known as living wills or advance directives. Even though at the time of writing no legislation specifically allows these documents, the courts have already accepted that individuals can refuse treatment or certain types of care or treatment in advance of that care or treatment being required, and that this can be done in writing.

These documents can be designed to suit the needs of individuals. They ordinarily set out the circumstances under which they will take effect, such as, "If I am terminally ill and there is no hope of recovery and I am not mentally capable of consenting to my own medical care . . ." They then direct that certain forms of care or treatment will not be given, such as cardiac or respiratory resuscitation, or extraordinary care.

These directions are in the negative. They are refusals of care. They cannot direct and bind physicians to perform certain types of care, just as a patient cannot force a physician to perform certain treatments in usual circumstances.

The problem with introducing legislation is that it would invariably outline a particular format to be followed. This would result in documents that might not be respected if the format was not followed. Under existing legal circumstances, as long as the language is clear, individuals are given far more latitude.

The major problem with living wills and advance directives is that if a patient arrives in a hospital and no one knows that the patient has refused certain types of care under specified circumstances, the staff will carry out whatever they feel is reasonable in the circumstances. It is therefore important for people who have made out such documents to give copies to family members and their family physician. In some cases, it might even be advisable to carry the directive on their person. This is the practice followed by Jehovah's Witnesses with respect to their advance directives regarding blood transfusions and the use of blood products.

Euthanasia

In the past number of years numerous stories have been widely reported in the press about the practice of euthanasia — that is, physicians putting patients to death. In any discussion of this highly emotional topic, it is necessary to define two terms.

The first is active euthanasia. This is the act of a physician or anyone else intended specifically to end the life of another human being. Under Canadian law this is a criminal offence. The killing of another person that is planned and deliberate is classified, under section 231 of the Criminal Code, as first degree murder, the punishment for which is life imprisonment. Even if the patient consents, active euthanasia is illegal.

The second is passive euthanasia. This is usually defined as an act that brings about the death of the patient but that is not directly intended for that purpose. Withdrawing of life supports, for instance, that are no longer reasonable to maintain is passive euthanasia. Providing drugs for the purpose of easing a patient's pain but which eventually bring about death is also passive euthanasia if the primary purpose of the treatment is not to end the life of the patient. Passive euthanasia is therefore legal in Canada, as long as it is reasonable in the circumstances. Preferably the patient has consented to it, or someone on behalf of the patient when the patient is not capable of consenting.

Suicide

Every so often suicide becomes a public issue, as it did in the case of Sue Rodriguez, of Victoria, B.C., in 1994. Mrs. Rodriguez, a 43-year-old wife and mother, suffered from Lou Gehrig disease (ALS, or amyotrophic lateral sclerosis). In the late stages of this incurable wasting disease, the patient cannot swallow, speak or move, but remains intellectually competent and aware.

Under Canadian law, attempted suicide is not a crime. However, section 241 of the Criminal Code makes counselling, aiding or abetting suicide a criminal offence, regardless of whether the attempted suicide is successful.

The result of this legislation is that as long as a person is mentally and physically able to obtain the means — the gun, the knife, the drugs — and able to use it to commit suicide, there are no criminal sanctions, even if the attempt is unsuccessful. Yet a person who wishes advice on how to commit suicide so as to bring about death in a swift and painless manner cannot get it, because anyone who provides such advice, let alone provides the means, is guilty of a criminal offence. The punishment is a maximum of fourteen years' imprisonment. The law clearly discriminates against those who are unable to commit suicide on their own.

A further anomaly is that a physician whose duty it is to aid in removing pain and suffering is not permitted to advise, let alone assist in, suicide, even if that is the only way the pain and suffering can be removed.

Mrs. Rodriguez appealed to the Supreme Court of Canada, asking it to allow her to have the right to a doctor to assist her suicide. The court decided she did not have that right. Her right to life, liberty and security of the person under the Canadian Charter of Rights and Freedoms was rejected. The court instead said that such a matter was in effect not their department and that Parliament should deal with the issue. One wonders how often the principles of law must win out over the needs of the suffering.

Durable or Enduring Power of Attorney

A second cousin to the living will is the durable, or enduring, power of attorney. This document is similar to an ordinary power of attorney in that one person gives to another the authority to act on their behalf. The authority of the "attorney" or agent is limited by the document. The problem is that when the principal (the person who signed the document) becomes mentally incompetent, the power of attorney ordinarily becomes invalid.

To rectify this problem, Nova Scotia, Quebec, Manitoba and Ontario have enacted legislation that allows a person to complete a power of attorney appointing another to make medical decisions on their behalf if they are no longer capable of making these decisions. To be valid, these documents must conform to the requirements of the legislation. The result is that there are differences from province to province. This creates great difficulty if a person from one province with a durable power of attorney moves to or becomes seriously ill in a province that does not have such legislation or whose legislation differs.

The durable power of attorney can simply appoint an agent, who would appear to be given complete discretion in making decisions. However, the Supreme Court of Canada, in the case of *Re Eve,* restricted the right of a mother of a retarded daughter to exercising decisions that were for the medical benefit of the daughter. In that case, the mother was not permitted to consent to the daughter's sterilization, because it was not considered medically necessary. A similar restriction could be placed on an agent under a durable power of attorney, though the matter has not been dealt with in the courts.

The person making a power of attorney can also restrict the authority of the agent. In this way, it can be combined with a living will or advance directive. The agent can be appointed to consent to or refuse certain types of care, such as life supports, under certain circumstances when the principal is no longer mentally able to make these decisions. Any agent appointed under a durable power of attorney has no more legal right than the patient has. Therefore, the agent cannot demand any particular care or treatment that the patient would not be able to demand. The agent could not, for instance, demand that a patient be kept on life supports when the patient is brain dead. The agent could not insist that the hospital continue to resuscitate the patient when resuscitation is not working and cardiac or respiratory arrests continue to occur, thus making resuscitation an unreasonable form of care.

In a province that does not have legislation allowing for a durable power of attorney, it is questionable whether such a document would have any legal authority. However, many hospitals might regard it in a favourable light and at least consult with the person who holds such a power of attorney.

The real problem arises when the person who holds a power of attorney in a province that does not recognize such a document is not the person who would ordinarily make decisions for a patient who is no longer mentally capable of making medical decisions. A parent of an unmarried adult would usually make such decisions. If a durable power of attorney is given to a friend, though, this presents the hospital with a dilemma. If there is legislation allowing for the document, it is clear that the person who holds it makes the decisions, not a parent, spouse, child or sibling.

Because of these uncertainties, it would appear that a living will or advance directive is a more workable solution. Then, the person drafting the document gives specific directions as to what care can or cannot be given. This denial of certain types of care must be respected. An agent to make these decisions may not be appointed unless such an appointment is allowed in the particular province and is written in the form that the legislation requires.

Before drafting a power of attorney or living will, it is clearly wise to seek legal advice.

Summary of Principles

1. Death is a condition of the human body to be determined by physicians who are trained to diagnose conditions of the body.

2. If there is a dispute as to when or if death occurred, the courts will balance the evidence given by witnesses as in the determination of any other fact.

3. The law does not tell doctors when the diagnosis of death is to be made.

4. The diagnosis of death is important because various legal rights and duties of the deceased end, and various legal rights and duties of others may arise as a result of wills, insurance, contracts or legislation.

5. There is no legal right to die, though there is a right to refuse care or treatment even though it may result in death.

6. There is a right to live, but not to require doctors and hospitals to provide unreasonable or unavailable care or treatment in order to sustain life.

7. Active euthanasia, the intentional killing of a patient, is a criminal offence in Canada, even if it is done to end pain and suffering of a patient, or if the patient is dying in any case, and even if the patient consents to the act.

8. Passive euthanasia, the intentional withdrawal of care and treatment or the failure to provide certain types of care and treatment, is legal in Canada, if providing that care and treatment is unreasonable. The consent of the patient is not required.

9. Providing drug therapy for the purpose of controlling pain is legal in Canada even though the therapy may hasten the death of the patient.

10. Attempted suicide in Canada is legal.

11. Aiding, counselling or abetting suicide in Canada is a criminal offence, even when it is done with the consent of the patient and for the purpose of ending pain and suffering.

12. Canadians have the right to have living wills or advance directives, even without provincial legislation, in which certain types of
care or treatment are refused in writing in advance if certain circumstances come about and the person is not mentally capable of making such decisions at the time.

13. In some provinces it is permissible to have a durable or enduring
power of attorney, in which a person appoints someone else to make
medical decisions on his or her behalf if the person appointing this
agent becomes mentally incapable of making those decisions.

24

AFTER
YOU'VE
GONE

GIVEN THE CONSTANT and often emotional debates over "whose body is it?" many people seem to think that someone owns their body. The issue arises in discussions of consent to treatment, abortions and the use or disposition of a body after death. In fact, people do not own their bodies in the way they own houses, cars and Canada Savings Bonds. During life, people have the right to control their bodies, and even that is restricted. For example, it is forbidden to put narcotics into one's body for non-medical use, and it is illegal to consent to being murdered. After death, a body still cannot be owned, sold or held for unpaid debts. It is not considered property. However, a human body is subject to various rights and responsibilities.

While a human being is still alive, that person has the legal right to give permission to others to deal with his or her body after death in a particular way. Those who have been given the responsibility of handling the deceased person's property after death — that is, the executors of the estate or the family — have the legal responsibility to dispose of the body. A problem arises when no one claims the remains. Traditionally, the community, usually the municipality, had the responsibility to provide for burial. Provincial legislation also provides for unclaimed bodies, in which a public official is given permission to make the necessary arrangements or to deliver the body to a medical school for the study of anatomy.

Directions while Alive
While a person is still alive, provincial legislation permits that person to give directions regarding the disposition of the body after death. These directions are usually not made part of the will, since by the time the will is found and opened it is often too late to follow the directions.

Every province has legislation that allows a person over the age of majority (which varies from province to province) to consent to the use of his or her body after death for therapeutic purposes; that is, for the treatment of someone else, for medical education or for scientific research. This legislation authorizes what are known as organ or tissue donations. Under this legislation, the person may consent or authorize that various parts of the body be removed and transplanted into another person. (Transplantation of the heart, lungs, kidneys and liver can save lives.) The consent can be either for specific organs or for transplantation in general. It can also be for donation of the entire body for academic or scientific purposes. Some donors consent specifically "for transplantation only," whereas others may leave the purpose open. Usually, no recipient is specified. Such consent must follow the format outlined in the provincial legislation. It usually must be given in writing, or orally during the person's last illness in the presence of two witnesses. If consent was given in one province and death occurred in another province, the consent would most likely be accepted, unless it did not meet the requirements of the legislation where death took place. Most provinces have similar legislation, so this is not likely to be a problem.

Because an organ or tissue donation is not really a donation, there is no requirement on anyone who receives the remains to use them for the purposes outlined, though they cannot use them for purposes to which the donor has not consented. For example, a person may "leave" his or her body to a particular medical school for research or study, but the medical school is not bound to accept the body. Similarly, donating a vital organ does not mean that it will be used. There may be no requirement at the time for that organ or it may not be in a suitable condition for transplantation.

For a transplant to be effective, it is vital that people who consent to an organ donation advise their family, their attending physician and the health facility in which they may be treated, so that the organ can be removed immediately after death. Otherwise, it is useless.

In most provinces, legislation permits the consent of the deceased to be binding, which means that the family of the deceased cannot object and overrule it. However, many health facilities are reluctant to proceed with the use of body parts over the objections of family. No one is required by law to follow the directions of the deceased if no legal duties are broken.

The direction of a deceased for the use of remains may also be prevented if the death falls within the authority of a coroner or medical examiner, in which case it would have to give way to a medico-legal investigation or at least the permission of the coroner or medical examiner to proceed with the use of the remains.

Once consent for the use of remains has been given, it can be withdrawn by the person who gave it. No one is then permitted to act on a prior consent.

Autopsies

There are two types of autopsies that may be performed on a human body. The first is conducted in a hospital or by a laboratory associated with the hospital. The purpose of this examination is to determine the cause of death and learn whether deaths of this sort could be prevented. It also may assist in the compilation of statistics to determine whether there are certain trends in causes of death in the community.

It is accepted practice that a certain number of hospital autopsies should take place as part of the attempt to maintain proper standards.

Just as a person may direct that parts of the body or the entire body may be used for various purposes after death, a similar direction authorizing the use of the body for scientific research and study includes the hospital autopsy. If the deceased has not given directions, the family may give the necessary consent.

Just as in a valid informed consent to treatment, the person giving the consent (or the family if the deceased has not consented) must be informed of the nature of the procedure. It must be understood that the body will be opened and various organs may be removed for examination and laboratory analysis. The body will then be removed to the funeral establishment designated by the family. Ordinarily, care will be taken in opening the body of a female not to leave the sewn-up incision visible if the remains are to be displayed in a low-cut dress. If there are plans for such display, specific instructions should be given to the hospital that no trace of the autopsy is to be visible above the breast line. These instructions should be given in writing as a condition on the consent-to-autopsy form.

The hospital should be advised if an open-casket funeral is to take place, with a condition being added to the consent that the body will not be altered in any way that would make this impossible. The hospital can then decide whether it wishes to proceed in light of these restrictions.

Autopsies that include opening the skull are ordinarily performed in such a way that the scalp is replaced over the opening, leaving no indication of the examination. If for some reason the face is to be altered, the family should be made aware of it. Before consenting to the autopsy, a discussion should be held with the funeral director, who can advise what limitations there may be in placing a body on view.

Despite great pressure that may be placed on a family, it should be noted that there is no legal requirement that forces a family to consent to a hospital autopsy.

Medico-Legal Investigations
There are situations in which the death of an individual is not simply a private affair. The public and, therefore, the public authorities have an interest and an involvement. These situations arise when

the death has been caused by negligence, violence or foul play, or there is no known cause of death. In these situations the community as a whole is concerned about the loss of one of its members and wishes to have the death investigated and the cause of death determined. It is also interested in learning whether the death could have been avoided, or whether similar deaths could be prevented in the future.

To satisfy this public interest, every province has a coroner or, in Alberta, Manitoba and Nova Scotia, a medical examiner. By provincial or territorial legislation, this official is given the responsibility to investigate certain types of death.

Under the legislation, there is a duty on everyone who has reason to believe that the death was or may have been caused by one of the possible causes listed in the legislation to notify the coroner or medical examiner. These causes, which differ from province to province, include violence, misadventure, negligence, misconduct and malpractice, as well as death during or following pregnancy, death that occurs suddenly or unexpectedly, death from a disease or illness that was not being treated by a physician, and when the deceased was an in-patient in specific institutions such as a psychiatric hospital or jail.

Once the coroner or medical examiner has been notified, the family loses the right to possess the remains. That official takes control, conducts an investigation and may conduct an autopsy. An inquest or fatality inquiry may be ordered or recommended, depending on the province in which the death took place and the requirements of the legislation. When the body is no longer needed, it is returned to the family for disposal.

If an inquest or inquiry is held, it is important for the family to seek legal advice. The inquest conducted by the coroner (or, in the medical examiner system, an inquiry by a judge) is a hearing to determine the cause of death. Often this step is taken because the investigation and autopsy could not determine the cause of death.

The inquest or inquiry is not a trial. There are no parties as in a lawsuit. Lawyers may be permitted to represent those who have an interest in the matter, but no one has a right to appear or to call and cross-examine witnesses.

Witnesses can be ordered to attend, though many of the rights they have in an ordinary court do not apply.

At the conclusion there is a finding and often a series of recommendations. No one is ordered to make a payment or to be punished. However, the finding may reflect adversely on the family or others. It may be that the deceased died as a result of family neglect or by the negligence of a hospital. These findings do not bind any court but they can provoke a lawsuit, disciplinary action or a criminal prosecution. For this reason, those who may be involved should be represented by legal counsel in order to argue against the possibility of such a verdict.

Arrangements for Disposition

In preparing for death, many patients consider having a durable power of attorney or a living will. (See chapter 23, "Dying and Death.") In addition, many patients consider how their remains are to be handled after death. Directions regarding funeral arrangements and disposition, whether included in the will or set out separately, are not binding on the family or executors.

However, many patients make arrangements in advance and pay for them, so that the executors are most likely to follow them. The first decision to be made is to choose a funeral director to handle the remains. The patient should meet with the funeral director to discuss the various options. That a funeral director is involved does not mean that traditional funeral ceremonies have to be held. The funeral director will make arrangements for the removal of the remains from wherever the death took place and will ensure that the death certificate is completed and that a burial permit or other permit is obtained.

In some cases a person wishes to have the remains immediately cremated without being on display or without being present at a funeral. On the other hand, if the body is to be on display or present, a casket will have to be purchased. Crematoria ordinarily require some type of casket for the purpose of handling the remains. Some funeral homes will rent caskets for display only. Following the viewing, arrangements must be made.

Arrangements for final disposition may be made with the assistance of the funeral director, but if burial of the remains is to take place, or burial of an urn of ashes after cremation, separate discussions will be necessary with a cemetery or mausoleum.

It is possible to prepare funeral homes for whatever services are requested. These funds are kept in trust by the funeral home in order to provide the services at a particular quality when death occurs. Ordinarily, the purchase of an actual casket does not take place, since it would have to be stored until death occurs. Pre-need arrangements usually guarantee a casket of a particular standard.

Care must be taken to ensure that it is clearly understood whether the amount paid will cover all of the services purchased, or whether the estate will have additional costs. The issue of whether the family can make any changes in the arrangements should also be discussed, as well as whether there will be any refund if not all the arrangements are followed.

Summary of Principles

1. A patient has no right to leave his or her body in a will but can under provincial legislation, such as human tissue gift legislation, direct and authorize that it be used for transplantation, research or education.

2. There is no duty on anyone to follow the direction given by a deceased regarding the use of the body, but no one may exceed the authorization given, unless provincial legislation permits it.

3. Surviving family members can overrule the directions of the deceased only if provincial legislation under which the direction was given permits it.

4. If the death falls within the authority of the coroner or medical examiner, a medico-legal autopsy can be performed without the consent of any other person, regardless of the desires of the deceased, the surviving family or the executors of the estate.

5. A person has the right to prepay and make pre-need arrangements with a funeral establishment for the disposition of the remains, though the executors of the estate and the family are not bound by the arrangements.

ADDITIONAL READING

In the late 1970s, Canada had produced less than a handful of books on the subject of health law. Now there are at least a couple of dozen on various aspects of the subject. The following list is a selection. It is by no means complete, but it does include various reports produced by law reform bodies and task forces. Most of these are published by law publishers and are not ordinarily found on the bookshelves of public bookstores. They may be ordered directly from the publishers or through bookstores. Some are available in public libraries, law libraries, hospital libraries and libraries connected with schools for the training of various health disciplines such as nursing. There are few books on health law published in Canada specifically for the public.

In addition, numerous articles on health law have appeared in law journals across Canada. These journals are found in law libraries.

Health law problems are not unique to Canada. The United States produces hundreds of books on the subject, with occasional books coming from other countries such as Britain. Many of the problems discussed are the same as those found in Canada. However, the legal solutions are not always the same. Great care must be taken by the reader who is not legally trained. The reader should not assume that the approach of courts in the United States and Britain will necessarily be the same as those in Canada, even though there may be many similarities.

In researching the subject, you may find books and articles that discuss patient rights under the older titles of forensic medicine, medical law or medico-legal. The more current title used, however, is health law.

1. The Right to Health Care
Arthur J. Meagher, Peter J. Marr and Ronald A. Meagher, *Doctors and Hospitals: Legal Duties* (Toronto: Butterworths, 1991) Chap. 2, 7

2. The Right to a Doctor of One's Choice
Gilbert Sharpe, *The Law & Medicine in Canada, 2nd ed.* (Toronto: Butterworths, 1987) Chap. 14

J.J. Morris, *Law for Canadian Health Administrators* (Toronto: Butterworths, 1994)

4. Consent to Treatment
Arthur J. Meagher, Peter J. Marr and Ronald A. Meagher, *Doctors and Hospitals: Legal Duties* (Toronto: Butterworths, 1991) Chap. 5, 6

J.J. Morris, *Canadian Nurses and the Law* (Toronto: Butterworths, 1991) Chap. 8

J.J. Morris, *Law for Canadian Health Administrators* (Toronto: Butterworths, 1994)

Lorne E. Rozovsky, *Canadian Dental Law* (Toronto: Butterworths, 1987) Chap. 3

Lorne E. Rozovsky and Fay A. Rozovsky, *The Canadian Law of Consent to Treatment* (Toronto: Butterworths, 1990)

Gilbert Sharpe, *The Law & Medicine in Canada, 2nd ed.* (Toronto: Butterworths, 1987) Chap. 4

5. Negligence and Standards of Care
Arthur J. Meagher, Peter J. Marr and Ronald A. Meagher, *Doctors and Hospitals: Legal Duties* (Toronto: Butterworths, 1991) Chap. 3, 4, 7
J.J. Morris, *Canadian Nurses and the Law* (Toronto: Butterworths, 1991) Chap. 9
Ellen I. Picard, *Legal Liability of Doctors and Hospitals in Canada, 2nd ed.* (Toronto: Carswell, 1984) Chap. 4
Lorne E. Rozovsky, *Canadian Dental Law* (Toronto: Butterworths, 1987) Chap. 1
Gilbert Sharp, *The Law & Medicine In Canada, 2nd ed.* (Toronto: Butterworths, 1987) Chap. 3

6. Who Is Responsible for Whom?
Arthur J. Meagher, Peter J. Marr and Ronald A. Meagher, *Doctors and Hospitals: Legal Duties* (Toronto: Butterworths, 1991) Chap. 11, 16

7. Treatment of Children
Lorne E. Rozovsky and Fay A. Rozovsky, *The Canadian Law of Consent to Treatment* (Toronto: Butterworths, 1990)

9. Patient Records, Access and Confidentiality
Arthur J. Meagher, Peter J. Marr and Ronald A. Meagher, *Doctors and Hospitals: Legal Duties* (Toronto: Butterworths, 1991) Chap. 10, 12

J.J. Morris, *Canadian Nurses and the Law* (Toronto: Butterworths, 1991) Chap. 5
J.J. Morris, *Law for Canadian Health Administrators* (Toronto: Butterworths, 1994)
Lorne E. Rozovsky, *Canadian Dental Law* (Toronto: Butterworths, 1987) Chap. 5
Lorne E. Rozovsky and Fay A. Rozovsky, *AIDS and Canadian Law* (Toronto: Butterworths, 1992) Chap. 3
Lorne E. Rozovsky and Fay A. Rozovsky, *Canadian Health Information, 2nd ed.* (Toronto: Butterworths, 1992)

14. Sterilization
Competence and Human Reproduction, Report No. 52 (Edmonton, Alta.: Institute of Law Research and Reform, Feb. 1989)
Bartha M. Knoppers, *Human Dignity and Genetic Heritage,* Study paper (Ottawa: Law Reform Commission of Canada, 1991)
Sterilization Decisions: Minors and Mentally Incompetent Adults, Report for Discussion No. 6 (Edmonton, Alta.: Institute of Law Research and Reform, Mar. 1988)

15. Having a Baby by Technology
Medically Assisted Procreation, Working Paper 65 (Ottawa: Law Reform Commission of Canada, 1992)
Proceed with Care: Final Report of the Royal Commission on New Reproductive Technologies, (Ottawa: Minister of Government Services, 1993)

17. AIDS as a Communicable Disease

Lorne E. Rozovsky and Fay A. Rozovsky, *AIDS and Canadian Law* (Toronto: Butterworths, 1992)

18. Mental Illness

Gerald B. Robertson, *Mental Disability and the Law in Canada* (Toronto: Carswell, 1987) Chap. 14, 15

Harvey Savage and Carla McKague, *Mental Health Law in Canada* (Toronto: Butterworths, 1987)

22. Why Don't Patients Sue?

Pierre Deschamps, Kathleen C. Glass, Bartha M. Knoppers and Brigette Mornault, *Report on Health Care Liability in Canada* (Montreal: Quebec Research Centre of Private and Comparative Law, McGill University, 1989)

J. Robert S. Prichard, Chair, *Liability and Compensation in Health Care* (Toronto: University of Toronto Press, 1990)

23. Dying and Death

Euthanasia, Aiding Suicide and Cessation of Treatment, Report 20 (Ottawa: Law Reform Commission of Canada, 1982)

J.J. Morris, *Law for Canadian Health Administrators* (Toronto: Butterworths, 1994)

Lorne E. Rozovsky and Fay A. Rozovsky, *AIDS and Canadian Law* (Toronto: Butterworths, 1992) Chap. 15

Some Aspects of Medical Treatment and Criminal Law, Report 28 (Ottawa: Law Reform Commission of Canada, 1986)

24. After You've Gone

Procurement and Transfer of Human Tissues and Organs, Working Paper 66 (Ottawa: Law Reform Commission of Canada, 1992)

T. David Marshall, *Canadian Law of Inquests* (Toronto: Carswell, 1980)

J.J. Morris, *Law for Canadian Health Administrators* (Toronto: Butterworths, 1994)

APPENDICES

Notes

The following appendices list authorities to whom complaints can be made. It should be noted that this list is not complete. In many provinces, additional authorities exist for disciplines such as dietitians, massage therapists and medical radiation technologists. However, in other provinces, these disciplines are not licensed and therefore are not subject to any disciplinary proceedings under law. This list consists of those authorities that would be responsible for most complaints that might arise. If there are any doubts about the authority to which a complaint should be sent, contact the provincial Deputy Minister of Health.

APPENDIX A

Deputy Ministers

If in doubt as to where a complaint against a member of a health profession or any health services should be sent, refer the complaint to the Deputy Minister of Health of the province in which the person or service operates. Complaints against any of the following should also be sent to the provincial Deputy Minister of Health:

a. health services operated by the provincial department or Ministry of health;
b. hospitals;
c. nursing homes and other long term care facilities; and,
d. mental health centres.

Many provinces have combined social services and health under the same governmental department. As long as the complaint clearly specifies the services being complained about, it can be referred by the Deputy Minister of Health to the appropriate authority. Some services, such as home care, are currently in a state of flux. In many instances, there is no licensing authority and therefore, no one who is clearly responsible for handling complaints. Even in such cases, it is appropriate to complain to the Deputy Minister of Health.

Many public health services are operated by municipal boards of health. These boards operate under the authority of provincial legislation. It is therefore appropriate to send complaints about municipal health services to the provincial Deputy Minister of Health.

If a response is not received, or if the matter is not handled in a manner that the complainant feels is appropriate, the complaint should be sent to the Minister of Health with a copy to the Deputy Minister of Health.

BRITISH COLUMBIA
Deputy Minister of Health
1515 Blanshard Street
Victoria, British Columbia
V8W 3C8

ALBERTA
Deputy Minister
Alberta Health
18th Floor,
10025 Jasper Avenue
P.O. Box 2222
Edmonton, Alberta
T5J 2P4

SASKATCHEWAN
Deputy Minister of Health
T.C. Douglas Building
3475 Albert Street
Regina, Saskatchewan
S4S 6X6

MANITOBA
Deputy Minister of Health
Room 308, Legislative Building
Winnipeg, Manitoba
R3C 0V8

ONTARIO
Deputy Minister of Health
10th Floor, Hepburn Block
Queen's Park
Toronto, Ontario
M7A 1R3

QUÉBEC
Sous-ministre
Ministère de la Santé et des Services
sociaux
1075, chemin Sainte-Foy
Québec City, Québec
G1S 2M1

NEW BRUNSWICK
Deputy Minister
Department of Health and
Community Services
P.O. Box 5100
Fredericton, New Brunswick
E3B 5G8

NOVA SCOTIA
Deputy Minister
Department of Health
P.O. Box 488
Halifax, Nova Scotia
B3J 2R8

PRINCE EDWARD ISLAND
Deputy Minister
Department of Health and Social
Services
P.O. Box 2000
Charlottetown, P.E.I.
C1A 7N8

NEWFOUNDLAND
Deputy Minister
Department of Health
West Block,
Confederation Building
P.O. Box 8700
St. John's, Newfoundland
A1B 4J6

YUKON
Deputy Minister of Health and
Social Services
P.O. Box 2703
Whitehorse, Yukon
Y1A 2C6

NORTHWEST TERRITORIES
Deputy Minister of Health
P.O. Box 1320
Yellowknife, Northwest Territories
X1A 2L9

CANADA
Complaints to a federal Deputy
Minister should only be made about
services operated by that federal
department. The federal government has no authority to deal with
complaints about any individual
health professional or health institution other than complaints regarding
the conduct of its own employees.

Deputy Minister
Health Canada
Room 2140,
Jeanne Mance Building
Ottawa, Ontario
K1A 0L2

Deputy Minister
Veterans Affairs Canada
66 Slater Street
Ottawa, Ontario
K1A 0P4

Deputy Minister
Department of Citizenship and
Immigration
Place du Portage, Phase IV
Hull, Québec
K1A 0J9

Solicitor General
Correctional Services of Canada
340 Laurier Avenue West
Ottawa, Ontario
K1A 0P9

Appendix B

Provincial and Territorial Health Insurance Authorities

A complaint may be sent to the Deputy Minister of Health who can then refer it to the appropriate official. However, complaints can be expedited by sending them directly to the health insurance authority.

In these listings, "hospital insurance" refers to government health insurance for hospital services and "medical services insurance" refers to government health insurance for physicians' services. In some provinces, both services are operated by the same government agency, while in others, two separate agencies are involved. The authorities listed may also provide other types of health insurance, such as for drugs or dental services. However, complaints about private health insurance plans should not be made to these government agencies since they have no control over them. They should be made directly to the companies involved.

A. Hospital Insurance Authorities

BRITISH COLUMBIA
Assistant Deputy Minister
Institutional Services
Ministry of Health
1515 Blanshard Street, 5th Floor
Victoria, British Columbia
V8W 3C8

ALBERTA
Assistant Deputy Minister
Hospital Services Division
Alberta Health
10025 Jasper Avenue
P.O. Box 2222
Edmonton, Alberta
T5J 2P4

SASKATCHEWAN
Associate Deputy Minister
Integrated Services Branch
Department of Health
T.C. Douglas Building
3475 Albert Street
Regina, Saskatchewan
S4S 6X6

MANITOBA
Associate Deputy Minister
Hospitals and Community Health
Services
Manitoba Health
599 Empress Street
P.O. Box 925
Winnipeg, Manitoba
R3C 2T6

ONTARIO
Director
Institutional Health
Department of Health
10th Floor, Hepburn Block
80 Grosvenor Street
Toronto, Ontario
M7A 1R3

QUÉBEC
Directeur
Service à la clientèle
Régie de l'assurance-maladie du
Québec
1125, chemin Saint-Louis (56)
C.P. 6600
Québec City, Québec
G1K 7T3

NEW BRUNSWICK
Assistant Deputy Minister
Public Health and Medical Services
Department of Health and
Community Services
P.O. Box 5100
Fredericton, New Brunswick
E3B 5G8

NOVA SCOTIA
Administrator
Facilities Division
Department of Health
P.O. Box 488
Halifax, Nova Scotia
B3J 2R8

PRINCE EDWARD ISLAND
Manager
Health and Community Services
Agency
P.O. Box 3000
Montague, P.E.I.
C0A 1R0

NEWFOUNDLAND
Director
Hospital Services Division
Department of Health
Confederation Building
Higgins Line
P.O. Box 4750
St. John's, Newfoundland
A1C 5T7

YUKON
Director
Health Care Insurance
Department of Health and Social
Services
P.O. Box 2703
Whitehorse, Yukon
Y1A 2C6

NORTHWEST TERRITORIES
Director
Health Insurance Services
Department of Health
Government of the Northwest
Territories
P.O. Box 1320
Yellowknife, Northwest Territories
X1A 2L9

B. Medical Services Insurance
Authorities

BRITISH COLUMBIA
Chair
Medical Services Commission
Ministry of Health
1515 Blanshard Street, 5th Floor
Victoria, British Columbia
V8W 3C8

ALBERTA
Assistant Deputy Minister
Health Care Insurance Division
Alberta Health
10025 Jasper Avenue
P.O. Box 1360
Edmonton, Alberta
T5J 2N3

SASKATCHEWAN
Executive Director
Medical Care Insurance Branch
Department of Health
T.C. Douglas Building
3475 Albert Street
Regina, Saskatchewan
S4S 6X6

MANITOBA
Executive Director
Insured Benefits Branch
Manitoba Health
599 Empress Street
P.O. Box 925
Winnipeg, Manitoba
R3C 2T6

ONTARIO
Director
Ontario Health Insurance Plan
49 Place d'Armes
P.O. Box 48
Kingston, Ontario
K7L 5J3

QUÉBEC
Directeur
Service à la clientèle
Régie de l'assurance-maladie du
Québec
1125, chemin Saint-Louis (56)
C.P. 6600
Québec City, Québec
G1K 7T3

NEW BRUNSWICK
Assistant Deputy Minister
Public Health and Medical Services
Department of Health and
Community Services
P.O. Box 5100
Fredericton, New Brunswick
E3B 5G8

NOVA SCOTIA
Medical Director
Nova Scotia Medical Services
Insurance
P.O. Box 500
Halifax, Nova Scotia
B3J 2S1

PRINCE EDWARD ISLAND
Manager
Health and Community Services
Agency
P.O. Box 3000
Montague, P.E.I.
C0A 1R0

NEWFOUNDLAND
Executive Director
Newfoundland Medical Care
Commission
Elizabeth Towers, Elizabeth Avenue
P.O. Box 200
St. John's, Newfoundland
A1C 5J3

YUKON
Director
Health Care Insurance
Department of Health and Social
Services
P.O. Box 2703
Whitehorse, Yukon
Y1A 2C6

NORTHWEST TERRITORIES
Director
Health Insurance Services
Department of Health
Government of the Northwest
Territories
P.O. Box 1320
Yellowknife, Northwest Territories
X1A 2L9

APPENDIX C

Provincial Licensing Authorities for Ambulance Services

Not all provinces have licensing authorities for ambulance services. If no such authority exists, complaints should be sent to the Deputy Minister of Health.

BRITISH COLUMBIA
EMA Licensing Branch
Emergency Health Services
Commission
1515 Blanshard Street, 4th Floor
Victoria, British Columbia
V8W 3C8

ALBERTA
Emergency Health Services
Alberta Health
P.O. Box 1360
Edmonton, Alberta
T5J 2N3

SASKATCHEWAN
Emergency Medical Services
Saskatchewan Health
3475 Albert Street
Regina, Saskatchewan
S4S 6X6

MANITOBA
Emergency Services Branch
Manitoba Health
P.O. Box 925
599 Empress Street
Winnipeg, Manitoba
R3C 2T6

ONTARIO
Investigation and Licensing Service
Emergency Health Services Branch
Ministry of Health
5700 Yonge Street, 6th Floor
Toronto, Ontario
M2M 4K2

QUÉBEC
There are 18 regional licensing
authorities for ambulance services in
Québec. Complaints should be
referred to the licensing authority
for the region in which the service
was provided.

NEW BRUNSWICK
Ambulance Services Branch
Department of Health and
Community Services
P.O. Box 5100
Fredericton, New Brunswick
E3B 5G8

PRINCE EDWARD ISLAND
Ambulance Services Coordinator
Health and Community Services
Agency
4 Sydney Street
Charlottetown, P.E.I.
C1A 1E9

NEWFOUNDLAND
Board of Commissioners of Public
Utilities
P.O. Box 9188
St. John's, Newfoundland
A1A 2X9

APPENDIX D

Provincial Licensing Authorities for Chiropractors

BRITISH COLUMBIA
British Columbia College of
Chiropractors
7031 Westminister Highway, #102
Richmond, British Columbia
V6X 1A3

ALBERTA
College of Chiropractors of Alberta
216 Chinook Professional Blvd. S.W.
Calgary, Alberta
T2H 0K9

SASKATCHEWAN
The Chiropractors' Association of
Saskatchewan
200 - 514 Queen Street
Saskatoon, Saskatchewan
S7K 0M5

MANITOBA
Manitoba Chiropractors' Assn.
2706 - 83 Garry Street
Winnipeg, Manitoba
R3C 4J9

ONTARIO
College of Chiropractors of Ontario
130 Bloor Street West, #702
Toronto, Ontario
M5S 1N5

QUÉBEC
Ordre des chiropraticiens du
Québec
7950 boul. Metropolitain est
Ville d'Anjou, Québec
H1K 1A1

NEW BRUNSWICK
New Brunswick Chiropractors' Assn.
312 Main Street
Fredericton, New Brunswick
E3A 1E4

NOVA SCOTIA
Nova Scotia Chiropractic Assn.
65 Willow Street
Amherst, Nova Scotia
B4H 3W6

PRINCE EDWARD ISLAND
Prince Edward Island
Chiropractic Association
41 Pine Drive
Charlottetown, P.E.I.
C1A 6L6

NEWFOUNDLAND AND
LABRADOR
Newfoundland and Labrador
Chiropractic Association
760 Top Sail Road
Mount Pearl, Newfoundland
A1N 3J5

APPENDIX E

Provincial Licensing Authorities for Dentists

BRITISH COLUMBIA
College of Dental Surgeons of
British Columbia
500 - 1765 West 8th Avenue
Vancouver, British Columbia
V6J 5C6

ALBERTA
Alberta Dental Association
101 - 8230 105 Street
Edmonton, Alberta
T6E 5H9

SASKATCHEWAN
College of Dental Surgeons of
Saskatchewan
202 - 728 Spadina Crescent E.
Saskatoon, Saskatchewan
S7K 4H7

MANITOBA
Manitoba Dental Association
#103 - 698 Corydon Avenue
Winnipeg, Manitoba
R3M 0X9

ONTARIO
Royal College of Dental Surgeons of
Ontario
5th Floor, 6 Crescent Road
Toronto, Ontario
M4W 1T1

QUÉBEC
Ordre des dentistes du Québec
15e étage
625, boul. René-Lévesque Ouest
Montréal, Québec
H3B 1R2

NEW BRUNSWICK
New Brunswick Dental Society
Suite 11, 403 Regent Street
Fredericton, New Brunswick
E3B 3X6

NOVA SCOTIA
Provincial Dental Board of Nova
Scotia
5991 Spring Garden Road
Halifax, Nova Scotia
B3H 1Y6

PRINCE EDWARD ISLAND
Prince Edward Island Dental
Association
184 Belvedere Avenue
Charlottetown, P.E.I.
C1A 2Z7

NEWFOUNDLAND
Newfoundland Dental Board
211 LeMarchant Road
St. John's, Newfoundland
A1C 2H5

Provincial and Territorial Licensing Authorities for Denturists

BRITISH COLUMBIA
Dental Technicians and Denturists
Board of British Columbia
828 West 10th Avenue
Vancouver, British Columbia
V5Z 1L8

ALBERTA
Alberta Denturist Board of
Examiners
10011 - 109th Street, 5th Floor
Edmonton, Alberta
T5G 3S8

SASKATCHEWAN
Denturist Society of Saskatchewan
102 - 8th Street East
Saskatoon, Saskatchewan
S6V 0A7

MANITOBA
Denturist Association of Manitoba
Box 46105, Westdale P.O.
Winnipeg, Manitoba
R3R 3S3

ONTARIO
Ontario Governing Board of
Denture Therapists
1206 – 180 Bloor Street West
Toronto, Ontario
M5S 2V6

QUÉBEC
Ordre des denturologistes du
Québec
Bureau 106
45 Place Charles Lemoyne
Longueuil, Québec
J4K 5G5

NEW BRUNSWICK
New Brunswick Denturists Society
P.O. Box 128
Sussex, New Brunswick
E0E 1P0

NOVA SCOTIA
Denturist Licensing Board of Nova
Scotia
P.O. Box 935, Station M
Halifax, Nova Scotia
B3J 2V9

NEWFOUNDLAND
Newfoundland Denturists Board
23 St. Patricks Street
St. John's, Newfoundland
A1E 2S5

YUKON
Yukon Registrar of Denturists
Consumer & Corporate Affairs
Box 2703
Whitehorse, Yukon
Y1A 2C6

Appendix G

Provincial Licensing Authorities for Occupational Therapists

BRITISH COLUMBIA
British Columbia Society of
Occupational Therapists
c/o Victoria Office
4989 Prospect Lake Road
R.R. #7
Victoria, British Columbia
V8X 3X3

ALBERTA
Alberta Association of Registered
Occupational Therapists
#311, 4245 - 97 Street
Edmonton, Alberta
T6E 4Y7

SASKATCHEWAN
Saskatchewan Society of
Occupational Therapists
P.O. Box 9089
Saskatoon, Saskatchewan
S7K 7E7

MANITOBA
Association of Occupational
Therapy of Manitoba
320 Sherbrook Street at Portage
Winnipeg, Manitoba
R3B 2W6

ONTARIO
College of Occupational Therapy of
Ontario
700 Bay Street, 14th Floor
Box 333
Toronto, Ontario
M5G 1Z6

QUÉBEC
Corporation professionelle des
ergothérapeutes du Québec
1259, rue Berri, Suite 710
Montréal, Québec
H2L 4C7

NEW BRUNSWICK
New Brunswick Association of
Occupational Therapists
Georges Dumont Hospital
330 Archibald Street
Moncton, New Brunswick
E1C 2Z3

NOVA SCOTIA
Nova Scotia Association of
Occupational Therapists
5991 Spring Garden Road,
Suite 740
Halifax, Nova Scotia
B3H 1Y6

PRINCE EDWARD ISLAND
Prince Edward Island Association of
Occupational Therapists
P.O. Box 2248
Charlottetown, P.E.I.
C1A 8B9

NEWFOUNDLAND AND
LABRADOR
Newfoundland and Labrador
Occupational Therapy Board
P.O. Box 23076
St. John's, Newfoundland
A1B 4J9

Appendix H

Provincial Licensing Authorities for Optometrists

BRITISH COLUMBIA
Board of Examiners in Optometry
Province of British Columbia
P.O. Box 39502 Broadmoor P.O.
7940 Williams Road
Richmond, British Columbia
V7A 5G9

ALBERTA
Alberta College of Optometrists
Suite 905, 11830 Kingsway Avenue
Edmonton, Alberta
T5G 0X5

SASKATCHEWAN
Saskatchewan Association of
Optometrists
P.O. Box 967
North Battleford, Saskatchewan
S9A 2Z3

MANITOBA
Manitoba Association of
Optometrists
24 - 1st Avenue N.E.
Dauphin, Manitoba
R7N 1A4

ONTARIO
College of Optometrists of Ontario
6 Crescent Road
Toronto, Ontario
M4W 1T1

QUÉBEC
Ordre des optométristes du Québec
1326, rue Sherbrooke est
Montréal, Québec
H2L 1M2

NEW BRUNSWICK
Board of Examiners for New
Brunswick
CP 700/20, rue Victoria
Shediac, New Brunswick
E0A 3G0

NOVA SCOTIA
Board of Examiners
P.O. Box 970
Wolfville, Nova Scotia
B0P 1X0

NEWFOUNDLAND
Newfoundland Optometric Board
30 Commonwealth Avenue
Mount Pearl, Newfoundland
A1N 1W6

PRINCE EDWARD ISLAND
College of Optometrists of Prince
Edward Island
P.O. Box 906
Montague, P.E.I.
C0A 1R0

APPENDIX I

Provincial Licensing Authorities for Pharmacists

BRITISH COLUMBIA
College of Pharmacists of British
Columbia
#200 - 1765 West 8th Avenue
Vancouver, British Columbia
V6J 1V8

ALBERTA
Alberta Pharmaceutical Association
10130 - 112th Street, 7th Floor
Edmonton, Alberta
T5K 2K4

SASKATCHEWAN
Saskatchewan Pharmaceutical
Association
#700 - 4010 Pasqua Street
Regina, Saskatchewan
S4S 7B9

MANITOBA
Manitoba Pharmaceutical
Association
187 St. Mary's Road
Winnipeg, Manitoba
R2H 1J2

ONTARIO
Ontario College of Pharmacists
483 Huron Street
Toronto, Ontario
M5R 2R4

QUÉBEC
Ordre des pharmaciens du Québec
266, rue Notre-Dame Ouest
Bureau 301
Montréal, Québec
H2Y 1T6

NEW BRUNSWICK
New Brunswick Pharmaceutical
Society
Place Heritage Court
202 - 95 Foundry Street
Moncton, New Brunswick
E1C 5H7

NOVA SCOTIA
Nova Scotia Pharmaceutical Society
P.O. Box 3363 (S)
1526 Dresden Row
Halifax, Nova Scotia
B3J 3J1

PRINCE EDWARD ISLAND
Prince Edward Island Pharmacy
Board
P.O. Box 1084
Charlottetown, P.E.I.
C1A 7M4

NEWFOUNDLAND
Newfoundland Pharmaceutical
Association
Apothecary Hall
488 Water Street
St. John's, Newfoundland
A1E 1B3

Appendix J

Provincial and Territorial Licensing Authorities for Physicians

These are the authorities that license and discipline physicians. All complaints should be sent to them, and not to the provincial medical association or society which represents the interests of the medical profession and does not have the authority to discipline.

BRITISH COLUMBIA
College of Physicians and Surgeons
of British Columbia
1807 West 10th Avenue
Vancouver, British Columbia
V6J 2A9

ALBERTA
College of Physicians and Surgeons
of Alberta
900 Manulife Place
10180 - 101 Street
Edmonton, Alberta
T5J 4P8

SASKATCHEWAN
College of Physicians and Surgeons
of Saskatchewan
211 Fourth Avenue South
Saskatoon, Saskatchewan
S7K 1N1

MANITOBA
College of Physicians and Surgeons
of Manitoba
494 St. James Street
Winnipeg, Manitoba
R3G 3J4

ONTARIO
College of Physicians and Surgeons
of Ontario
80 College Street
Toronto, Ontario
M5G 2E2

QUÉBEC
Professional Corporation of
Physicians of Québec
1440 Ste.-Catherine West,
Ste. 914
Montréal, Québec
H3G 1S5

NEW BRUNSWICK
College of Physicians and Surgeons
of New Brunswick
1 Hampton Road
P.O. Box 628
Rothesay, New Brunswick
E0G 2W0

NOVA SCOTIA
Provincial Medical Board of Nova
Scotia
5248 Morris Street
Halifax, Nova Scotia
B3J 1B4

PRINCE EDWARD ISLAND
College of Physicians and Surgeons
of Prince Edward Island
199 Grafton Street
Charlottetown, P.E.I.
C1A 1L2

NEWFOUNDLAND
Newfoundland Medical Board
15 Rowan Street
St. John's, Newfoundland
A1B 2X2

YUKON
Government of Yukon
Consumer Services J-6
Box 2703
Whitehorse, Yukon
Y1A 2C6

NORTHWEST TERRITORIES
Medical Profession, Safety and
Public Services
Government of the Northwest
Territories
Yellowknife, Northwest Territories
X1A 2L9

Appendix K

Provincial Licensing Authorities for Physiotherapists

BRITISH COLUMBIA
Association of Physiotherapists and
Massage Practitioners
103 - 1089 West Broadway
Vancouver, British Columbia
V6H 1E5

ALBERTA
College of Physical Therapists of
Alberta
302 - 6020, 104th Street
Edmonton, Alberta
T6H 5S4

SASKATCHEWAN
Saskatchewan College of Physical
Therapy
Box 7385
Saskatoon, Saskatchewan
S7K 4J3

MANITOBA
Association of Physiotherapists of
Manitoba
719 - 167 Lombard Avenue
Winnipeg, Manitoba
R3R 0V3

ONTARIO
College of Physiotherapists of
Ontario
230 Richmond Street West,
10th floor
Toronto, Ontario
M5V 1V6

QUÉBEC
Corporation professionnelle des
physiothérapeutes du Québec
1100, avenue Beaumont
bureau 530
Ville Mont-Royal, Québec
H3P 3E5

NEW BRUNSWICK
New Brunswick Association of
Physiotherapists
440 Wilsey Road
Park Business Centre
Fredericton, New Brunswick
E3B 7G5

NOVA SCOTIA
Nova Scotia College of
Physiotherapists
5991 Spring Garden Road,
Ste. 740
Halifax, Nova Scotia
B3H 1Y6

PRINCE EDWARD ISLAND
Prince Edward Island College of
Physiotherapists
P.O. Box 3286
Charlottetown, P.E.I.
C1A 8W5

NEWFOUNDLAND AND
LABRADOR
Newfoundland & Labrador College
of Physiotherapists
P.O. Box 21351
St. John's, Nfld. A1A 5G6

APPENDIX L

Provincial and Territorial Licensing Authorities for Psychologists

BRITISH COLUMBIA
College of Psychologists of British
Columbia
#10, 865 West, 10th Avenue
Vancouver, B.C.
V5Z 1L7

ALBERTA
Professional Exam Office
8303 - 112 Street, Suite 740
Edmonton, Alberta
T6G 1K4

or

Psychologists Association of Alberta
Suite 400, 10123 - 99 Street
Edmonton, Alberta
T5J 3H1

SASKATCHEWAN
Saskatchewan Psychological
Association
Mental Health Centre
P.O. Box 1056
Weyburn, Saskatchewan
S4H 2L4

MANITOBA
Psychological Association of
Manitoba
1800 - 155 Carlton Street
Winnipeg, Manitoba
R3C 3H8

ONTARIO
Ontario Board of Examiners in
Psychology
1246 Yonge Street, Suite 201
Toronto, Ontario M4T 1W5

QUÉBEC
Corporation professionnelle des
psychologues du Québec
1100, avenue Beaumont
Ville Mont Royal
Montréal, Québec
H3P 3E5

NEW BRUNSWICK
College of Psychologists of
New Brunswick
P.O. Box 1194, Stn. A
Fredericton, New Brunswick
E3B 1B0

NOVA SCOTIA
Nova Scotia Board of Examiners in
Psychology
Ste. 1115, 5991 Spring Garden Rd.
Halifax, Nova Scotia
B3H 1Y6

PRINCE EDWARD ISLAND
Prince Edward Island Psychologists
Registration Board
c/o Department of Psychology
University of Prince Edward Island
Charlottetown, P.E.I.
C1A 4P3

NEWFOUNDLAND
Newfoundland Board of Examiners
in Psychology
P.O. Box 5666
Station C
St. John's, Newfoundland
A1C 5W8

NORTHWEST TERRITORIES
Registrar of Psychologists
Department of Safety & Public
Services
Government of Northwest
Territories
Yellowknife, Northwest Territories
X1A 2L9

APPENDIX M

Provincial and Territorial Licensing Authorities for Registered Nurses

In some instances, the disciplinary body is also the professional association
that represents the interests of its members. However, these associations
also have the additional responsibility of protecting the public through their
authority to discipline members. It should be noted that these organizations relate only to registered nurses. They do not have the authority to discipline other nursing professions, such as registered nursing assistants,
licensed practical nurses and certified nursing assistants, which have their
own disciplinary bodies.

BRITISH COLUMBIA
Registered Nurses Association of
British Columbia
2855 Arbutus Street
Vancouver, British Columbia
V6J 3Y8

MANITOBA
Manitoba Association of Registered
Nurses
647 Broadway Avenue
Winnipeg, Manitoba
R3C 0X2

ALBERTA
Alberta Association of Registered
Nurses
11620 - 168th Street
Edmonton, Alberta
T5M 4A6

ONTARIO
College of Nurses of Ontario
101 Davenport Road
Toronto, Ontario
M5R 3P1

SASKATCHEWAN
Saskatchewan Registered Nurses'
Association
2066 Retallack Street
Regina, Saskatchewan
S4T 2K2

QUÉBEC
Ordre des infirmières et infirmiers
du Québec
4200 ouest, boul. Dorchester
Montréal, Québec
H3Z 1V4

NEW BRUNSWICK
Nurses Association of New
Brunswick
165 Regent Street
Fredericton, New Brunswick
E3B 3W5

NOVA SCOTIA
Registered Nurses Association of
Nova Scotia
Suite 104,
120 Eileen Stubbs Avenue
Dartmouth, Nova Scotia
B3B 1Y1

PRINCE EDWARD ISLAND
Association of Nurses of Prince
Edward Island
P.O. Box 1838
Charlottetown, P.E.I.
C1A 7N5

NEWFOUNDLAND
Association of Registered Nurses of
Newfoundland
P.O. Box 6116
55 Military Road
St. John's, Newfoundland
A1C 5X8

YUKON
Yukon Registered Nurses
Association
P.O. Box 5371
Whitehorse, Yukon
Y1A 4Z2

NORTHWEST TERRITORIES
Northwest Territories Registered
Nurses Association
P.O. Box 2757
Yellowknife, Northwest Territories
X1A 2R1

Appendix N

Ombudsmen

Provincial ombudsmen have the authority to investigate complaints regarding government services, such as those operated by a provincial Ministry of Health. However, complaints should first be made to the Ministry or Department responsible. If the complaint is not handled satisfactorily, it is then appropriate to complain to the ombudsman.

In British Columbia, the
Ombudsman also has jurisdiction
over the professional licensing and
disciplinary bodies. It will investigate when the complainant is dissatisfied with the manner in which the
licensing and disciplinary body has
handled the original complaint.

BRITISH COLUMBIA
The Ombudsman
931 Fort Street
Victoria, British Columbia
V8V 3K3

or

The Ombudsman
202 - 1275 West 6th Avenue
Vancouver, British Columbia
V6H 1A6

INDEX

Nurses:
    doctor's responsibility, 65-68
    responsibility for, 63, 65-68
    responsibility of, 59-60, 68, 71

O
Occupational therapists, 229
Ombudsmen, 236
Optometrists, 230

P
Patient expectations, 191-192
Patient Records, 81-96
    access to by patient, 88-89
    access to by third parties, 89-92
    computerization of, 94-95
    correcting errors in, 92-93
    defamation in, 93-94
    ownership of, 87-88
    principles, summary of, 95-96
    purpose of, 81-83
    standards of, 83-87
Pharmacies, *see* Drug Stores
Pharmacists, complaints against, 231
Physicians, complaints against,
    232-233
Physiotherapists, 233-234
Post mortem examination, *see*
    Autopsy
Press, *see* Media
Property of patient:
    principles, summary of, 80
    responsibility for, 78-80
Psychiatric illness, *see* Mental illness
Psychologists, 234-235

R
Refusal of care, *see* Consent to
    treatment
Registered nurses, 235-236
Relations between doctors and
    patients, 97-100, 190-191
Research on patients, 150-153
    consent to, 151-152
    principles, summary of, 153

right to, 152-153
    standards of care in, 151
Records, *see* Patient Records
Reproduction, use of technology in,
    121-127
    artifical insemination by a donor
    123-124
    artifical insemination by the
    husband, 122-123
    in vitro fertilization, 125
    principles, summary of, 127
    surrogate motherhood, 125-127
Responsibility:
    divided, 68-69
    employee, 59-60
    for doctors, 62-64
    for employees, 60-62
    for nurses, 63, 65-68
    for patient's property, 78-80
    individual, 59-60
    master-servant rule, 60-62
    principles, summary of, 72
    shared, 68-69
    vicarious, 60-62
Right to health care, 1-4
    principles, summary of, 4

S
Sexual relations:
    doctor with patient, 97-100
    principles, summary of, 100
Standards of care:
    failure to meet, 44-45
    family physician *vs.* specialist, 56
    general practitioner *vs.* specialist, 56
    injury as result of failure to meet,
    51-52
    in performing abortion, 112-113
    in performing circumcision, 130
    in drug stores, 106-108
    in treatment of children, 73
    local differences, 55-56
    locality rule, 55-56
    mental illness and, 144
    of patient records 83-87